WHAT PEOPLE ARE SAYING
ABOUT THIS BOOK

"In *Never Give Up*, K.P. Yohannan shares the depths of pain and fear that he endured silently and the convictions our Lord gave him that carried him through them."

Dr. Bill Atwood
Anglican Bishop, USA

"K.P. sets out his flaws and weaknesses, his blessings and vision, his mistakes and failures, his joys and sorrows. Some of us get so caught in the decline and compromise of churches in our own cultural context that we lose sight of what Christ the King is doing around the world; Brother K.P. shakes us and wakes us."

Reverend Dr. Paul Blackham
Vicar of St. Crispin's Church, UK

"My heart was thoroughly moved as I read through this book of a man and his very personal journey the last several years."

Frank Bueckert
Pastor of Bergthaler Mennonite Church, Canada

"Every Christian who is dedicated to fulfilling a 'God-sized' vision needs the wisdom contained in these pages."

Troy Carl
President of International Scripture Ministries, USA

"This book is amazing. I believe it is needed as we face the tribulation period. Dr. Yohannan's sweet, humble spirit shines through like Noah's rainbow. I have been blessed by the book and others will be as well. Unless Jesus comes first, this book will be known as a Christian classic by future generations."

Pauline Cason
GFA World Supporter, USA

"K.P. Yohannan's love for the Lord shines beautifully through this book. In this book, he takes the reader into his most personal thoughts, theology, prayers and insights. Having traveled in South Asia on a vision tour with GFA World, we have seen firsthand . . . their heartfelt work."

Dave and Dodie Eyer
GFA World Supporters, Canada

"The use of personal experiences and biblical truths helps one walk away encouraged and confident in the power of God to overcome the darkness of the world."

Reverend Ryan Farrell
Pastor of Nackawic Wesleyan Church, Canada

"Dr. K.P. Yohanan has been a friend for many decades. His fresh and unique perspectives on perseverance will encourage you! . . . K.P. embodies perseverance in the power of faith."

Gino Geraci
Radio Talk Show Host on the Salem Network, USA

"In his latest book, *Never Give Up,* K.P. Yohannan takes us on an intimate journey through his greatest struggles, revealing God's power to transform our most terrible times into a testimony for His glory. This is a must read!"

Greg Gordon
Founder of SermonIndex.net, Canada

"God brings certain books and people into our lives precisely when we need them. *Never Give Up* is one of those books, and K.P. Yohannan is one of those people."

Hank Hanegraaff
President of the Christian Research Institute, USA

"Despite several years at the centre of a storm of controversy and attack, this book is not a self-justification but a remarkable testimony. What shines throughout the book is Dr. Yohannan's undimmed passion to make Christ known to all!"

Paul Harcourt
National Leader of New Wine, England

"I have known K.P. Yohannan for three decades. I have seen him in great triumph, and I watched him endure in great pain. His passion for the untold millions is undeniable, and his passion for honoring Christ is equally so. Though we both have taken different paths in our view of the church, K.P. has lived to please his Lord. This account in *Never Give Up* is brutally honest and refreshingly candid, and, therefore, helpful for anyone who wants to grow deeper."

Skip Heitzig
Senior Pastor of Calvary Albuquerque, USA

"In *Never Give Up*, we catch a glimpse into K.P. Yohannan's soul as he vulnerably pens some of the lessons he has learned. . . . There were several points when I had to put it down and have an honest talk with God. A worthwhile read."

Mark Hinde
Open Doors Scotland, UK

"This is a must read for every Christian leader facing spiritual attack."

Keith Knight
Executive Director of CCBF, Canada

"K.P. is a survivor, and, thank the Lord, he still has his hand on the plow. This book tells the tale of a man on mission. It is encouraging, emotional and excellent."

Chip Lusko
Pastor of Calvary Chapel, USA

"A testimony that will challenge your relationship with Jesus and encourage a deeper knowledge of the One who loves us so much He gave His life that we might be forever His—even in the dark times."

Tim Matthews
Africa Inland Mission International, UK

"This is a book full of joy, but it tells it like it is."

Reverend Canon John McGinley
New Wine, England

"Once again, K.P. Yohannan has caused us to think differently about things that we thought we always knew."

Reverend Johnnie Moore
President of Congress of Christian Leaders, USA

"Author K.P. Yohannan, with a level of gut-wrenching honesty and forthright transparency, shares the biblical and scriptural path to redemption and freedom only found in Jesus Christ. . . . Yohannan challenges all Christ followers of today to indeed never give up!"

Frank Sontag
Founder of KMG Ministries, USA

"There is something different about the countenance of those who have been through the fire, those who have walked through the valley of adversity. This is true of my friend K.P. Yohanan. *Never Give Up* is the story of a very personal journey."

Frank Wright, PhD
President and CEO of D. James Kennedy Ministries, USA

But in the end, it's only

a passing thing, *this shadow.*

Even darkness must pass.

a new day *will come.*

And when the sun shines,

it will shine out the clearer.

Those were the stories
that stayed with you …

Folk in those stories
had lots of chances of turning back,

only they didn't.

They kept going,
because they were holding on to something …

and it's worth fighting *for.*

— *The Lord of the Rings: The Two Towers* [1]

ALSO BY THE AUTHOR

Revolution in World Missions
No Longer a Slumdog
Come, Let's Reach the World
Living in the Light of Eternity
Touching Godliness
Destined to Soar
Dance Not for Time
Little Things that Make a Big Difference
Living by Faith, Not by Sight
Dependence Upon the Lord
A Life of Balance
Discouragement: Reasons and Answers

To read descriptions about materials above, or for a free download, please visit www.gfa.org/morebooks. To order you may also call a GFA World office near you.

NEVER

THE STORY OF A BROKEN MAN

GIVE

IMPACTING A GENERATION

UP

K.P. YOHANNAN

(Moran Mor Athanasius Yohan I, Metropolitan of Believers Eastern Church)

BOOKS

a division of GFA World

www.gfa.org

ISBN: 978-1-59589-175-4

Published by gfa books, a division of GFA World
1116 St. Thomas Way, Wills Point, TX 75169 USA
phone: (972) 300-7777
fax: (972) 300-7778

Printed in Canada

For more information about other materials, visit our website: www.gfa.org.

This book is **affectionately dedicated** *to those
who helped me survive this chaos.*

*To my wife, Gisela, and my son, Daniel,
who embraced my grief and pain in silence.*

*To my precious staff around the world, especially in the
U.S., who steadfastly stood with me during these years of
trial. Throughout this crisis, they each fought their own
battles, and only they know in full what that took.*

*To my dear friend and brother Francis Chan.
Thank you for being Christ to me during my journey
through the forest fire of grief.*

TABLE OF CONTENTS

FOREWORD

I have been inspired and challenged reading this powerful book by my brother in Christ and very dear friend, K.P. Yohannan. But for me this tells an even bigger story. It's an amazing account of God's hand upon the work K.P. Yohannan founded, which is now one of the largest ministries in the world. He is today probably our most famous OM graduate.

My relationship with him goes back over half a century. There are lots of memories during that span of time, but I especially remember him with the ship ministry when we were in Indonesia. I still have a photo of him sitting on the platform when we had a meeting in a huge stadium. Little did we know then what God had planned for him. I wish I had kept in better contact in those early years and been more of a help and blessing.

Then came his book, *Revolution in World Missions*,* dedicated to me. I found that some of what he wrote I disagreed with. We had an important meeting in Nepal, and he listened, and we came to an agreement and better understanding. Because of our conversation, he made some changes to the book. *Only* history will tell how much God has used his book, *Revolution in World Missions.*

I don't think you will understand what I am trying to say in this foreword if you have not read my latest book, *Messiology.*† You don't have to agree with all that he has written in this book to learn from it and enjoy it.

When K.P. Yohannan was brutally attacked in the media, I felt led to stand with him. He has always been willing to meet with me and pray with me and answer my questions. I heard his confessions and saw his humility and brokenness, and I knew the hand of the Lord was upon him. That is no small thing for me. I was grieved when Christians took him to court, which the Bible speaks against. Once that happens, everything becomes more complex, and you have to be careful about every word that comes out of your

---

* Available for free download at www.gfa.org.
† Available at Amazon.

mouth. It's a difficult path to find your way as you follow advice from professionals and listen to God and His Word. I felt articles in even the Christian press were often unfair and lacked facts and the big picture. It was difficult to watch.

If people could see what I have seen of the work of GFA, they would write differently. The work was, in fact, 10 times larger and deeper than I had imagined. Without question, GFA is one of the greatest works of God in our generation. The leadership team, called *episcopas* (bishops), is outstanding. This term is easily understood in the East. It's *not* the one-man show like many people imagine it to be, but I don't expect people to understand an Indian Apostle Paul of this generation.

K.P. Yohannan is an imperfect human being—but one with a pure heart, great passion and vision—indwelt by the Holy Spirit. You have a history-making, unique book in your hands, and I pray you will be blessed as you read this, and that it will help you along the road of your own life and ministry, especially in troubled times of your own.

George Verwer
Founder of Operation Mobilization International

THANK YOU

Thank you so much Jeena, Stephanie, Kendra, Teresa, David and Karen, for your hard work to get this manuscript ready. Thank you also to Nathan, Michelle, Susan, Carol and Keith, for the time and sacrifice you put into helping get this book ready to print, and to Lisa for the amazing work you did with the interior design. Thank you, Vanessa, for all you did in designing the beautiful cover. George Verwer, I can't thank you enough for writing the foreword for this book.

All glory to the Holy Trinity. Thank You for the awesome privilege I was given to see the Invisible through this journey of grief and fear.

INTRODUCTION

O ver a year ago, I felt the need to write this book. I dismissed the idea out of dread of reliving the grief and fear that filled four years in my journey, the part of it that I call "walking through the forest fire." But the feeling persisted and turned into a burden, which led me to pray and ask the Lord for His will and guidance.

This is how the writing of this book began.

One of the first instructions from the Lord was to read the second letter St. Paul wrote to the Corinthian Church and read it again and again until I understood the spirit in which he wrote it. I did not keep track of the number of times I read 2 Corinthians, but finally my heart saw, so vividly, *the heart of St. Paul* in writing that letter, and this is how the Lord led me to follow St. Paul's example in writing this book.

Please don't misunderstand me. I do not claim that what I write is inspired or supernatural. Rather, I found parallels of what I faced in Apostle Paul's writing. He had dealt with a situation similar to what I've been through recently—a season of criticism, misunderstanding, rejection, betrayal, accusation, and so on. But St. Paul, led by the Spirit of God, laid down his will to defend or respond to his critics as natural men would do. Instead, he chose to answer all their allegations by narrating his own journey of suffering and grief for the sake of His master. My whole world became brighter and more peaceful as I saw the way St. Paul responded to his critics and betrayers—and he did it with love and kindness.

Instead of focusing on the attacks he faced from people, he saw the bigger picture of the Holy Church and responded with pure love for his enemies. This way, then, became my model in writing this book.

Still, in my natural mind, I did have to understand how to take the dozen different tracks I wanted to follow, and yet have it be a cohesive whole leading to one destination. Having authored more than 275 books, I am not naïve about the roadmap to writing them. But this one is quite different from anything else I have written.

Now I understand why the Lord directed me to read 2 Corinthians countless times until I understood the spirit that moved St. Paul's writing. His personal life could not be separated from his passion for the Holy Church and from those who had never heard Christ's name.[1] And I realized, in the same way, my own personal journey cannot be separated from the world of the Holy Church and related matters that make sense of my life and the worldview I hold.

This book is a collection of my experiences and a reliving of events of these past few years in my journey with Christ and His Church.

This book is not an attempt to *defend* myself. I will leave that to the Lord. Rather, I offer to share what it was like to live through some incredibly difficult days, all the while growing in understanding how the Lord would use our struggle for the furtherance of His Kingdom, just as He has redeemed the struggles of His people time and time again since the beginning.

My prayer for this book is that my openness, sincerity and vulnerability will be an encouragement to you, dear reader, in your walk with God. I know that I am hardly the only Christ-follower to have had false information spread about them, so I trust that my carefully chosen words will provide hope to fellow wounded warriors.

I am also bold to believe that, through these pages, you will learn to find strength from the marvelous example of the early Church and the blueprint given to us in the Book of Acts.

I also hope that reading these pages will help you understand the ministry of GFA and the incredible work God is doing through our brothers and sisters around the world in these last days.

Finally, I want this book to convey a message of deep gratitude to the countless individuals and numerous congregations around the world that chose to believe the best about this all-too-human follower of Christ and the work He has called us to do.

And for all of us, the finish line is in sight. *Let's never give up.*

CHAPTER ONE

CAST INTO CHAOS

Live in faith and hope, though it be in darkness,
for in this darkness God protects the soul.
— St. John of the Cross[1]

It had been an ordinary day until that moment. My phone beeped, and I saw that I'd been sent a link. I clicked on it, as I usually do, and that was when everything stopped being usual and ordinary. My heart began to pound.

It was a report that one of the world's largest mission agencies was starting to collapse. Accusations of financial mismanagement, donor deception, negligent board oversight and more filled the screen. But what made it all the more devastating was that *I* was the one being written about, and it was *our mission*—GFA World—that was in the crosshairs.

I remember that moment, I couldn't even fathom what I could have done to merit such an attack. From the beginning, in my mind, these allegations were all false and unfounded.

A thousand thoughts overwhelmed me. They were not well-organized insights; rather, they were a jumble of disorganization. It was like bedlam in my mind.

Until that day, my life had been busy but manageable. But now chaos marked my life. Never had I experienced something so disruptive. And unfortunately, that first link I clicked wouldn't be the last such article to negatively impact my life and the ministry the Lord had entrusted to me. Little did I know that I was at the beginning of a valley of chaos and turmoil, my test that would last for what would feel like forever.

✠ ✠ ✠

Chaotic behavior exists in numerous natural systems. An example would be weather patterns. For the most part they are predictable—but never with perfect precision. That's because even small changes in data can have a profound effect on an eventual outcome.

Unexpected, chaotic incidents affect people every day. Your healthy young husband or father is diagnosed as having an aggressive lymphoma, and he is gone just a few months later.

You have your ideal job. Then one day you are unexpectedly called into your boss's office and informed that it is over, just like that.

You win all kinds of awards for your aggressive style of play . . . then an injury changes everything, including the trajectory of your life.

You discover your best friend has betrayed you. You are devastated.

Coming home on the expressway, a tire blows on your car, and you are the cause of a multi-auto accident. You cause irreversible harm to others and yourself, in mind and body.

Someone you trusted too much robs you of your life savings and vanishes.

Or you begin to realize that a group of people, for whatever their reasons, is determined to strip you of your reputation and ministry, and, apparently, they will stop at nothing as they pursue their goal.

It takes a while to wrap your head around it and to realize that everything about how you live your life must change before you can even start to respond to such situations.

But it didn't take long to understand that what we were facing at GFA was not an attack of flesh and blood, but of the powers of darkness.[2] Having faced numerous complicated situations in the past, I assumed this was another similar problem to deal with. When you are the founder of a missions movement that is scattered throughout the world, crossing hundreds of cultures, involving people groups with well over 300 languages, one can only imagine the complexity of dealing with the ever-changing nature of such an experience. Falling back on well-learned patterns, I said to myself, *Trust in the Lord. Mobilize prayer and keep the focus on bringing Christ's love to this desperate and hungry world.* And that's what I determined to do.

In retrospect, I was naïve. I hadn't yet realized the size and scope and craftiness of the assault gathering against us. This was not to be a one-and-done attack. Large and relentless, these negative forces quickly established an ever-increasing momentum that proved next to impossible to stop.

Our staff were inundated with phone calls about these charges as the article and other accusations spread. More letters needed to be answered than could be managed by our qualified workers. Accusations from hostile bloggers were quoted (would you believe) even in religious publications. Negative news articles were written and published without an attempt to hear our side of the story. It felt like I was living in a nightmare with no way to wake up.

I must not get bogged down by these distractions, I told myself. As Robert Frost wrote, "But I have promises to keep, And miles to go before I sleep . . . ."[3] That's the attitude I attempted to maintain. So, I kept on traveling to the many countries where we minister, just as St. Paul did in the days of the early Church. I still had to lead my team and the countless believers God has entrusted to us. I had no choice. My schedule was full.

✝ ✝ ✝

I boarded yet another 20-hour flight from Dallas, Texas, that would take me to a remote part of the great land of India where I was born and raised. It is an amazing country with beautiful people, many of whom now love the Lord.

Finally, I arrived at the southern point of the country. This is where the St. Thomas Community and the global headquarters of Believers Eastern Church is located. Believers Eastern Church (BEC) is the massive church movement that was born as the result of doing missions, following the same pattern as what was recorded in St. Matthew 28:19–20 and Acts 13.

I was so glad to be back in my home country and community. How nice it would be to lie down in my own bed and rest for a day or so before getting into the battle again! The wooden leaves of my favorite Hunter ceiling fan turned ever so slowly and silently above my bed. This old, one-bedroom house was built 260 years ago by skilled carpenters. It is all made of wood—walls, ceilings, roof and floor. I imagine simple chisels and a wooden hammer were the tools used to construct it. This 1,800-square-foot house has a 45-degree pitched roof, and it's beautiful.

This home is the official residence (officially called *aramana,* a name used by eastern churches in this part of the world) of the Metropolitan of Believers Eastern Church. The title *Metropolitan* is a term used to describe the head bishop of a church. (I will share with you a little later how I came to hold this position). The Metropolitan is considered the first among equals, and he works together with a team of other bishops to lead the church, just as bishops have been doing since the beginning of the Holy Church.

When I am no longer serving as the Metropolitan, this house and all its contents will pass on to the person who takes my place. It belongs fully to the church, not to me.

The house sits about a quarter of a mile from the Believers Eastern Church global headquarters (the Synod Secretariat) where oversight is given to all the church's administrative regions, or dioceses, scattered throughout the world. The Synod Secretariat is located on our 180-acre wooded church property, filled with so many kinds of flowers and plants and more than 350 different kinds of wild birds. Everywhere you look you see rolling hills with winding roads. Walk a little further and you come upon our 11-acre lake, filled 30–65 feet deep with clean, pure water, which freely provides water to the entire community and all the staff and seminary students who reside there. The centerpiece of our community is St. Thomas Believers Eastern Church Cathedral where our daily prayer meetings and various services take place. The entire campus is purposely set apart from the chaos of the world to promote a quiet and meditative atmosphere, designed to direct all attention to God.

It is late at night, and I'm jetlagged because I have flown from the other side of the globe. Yet I am unable to sleep. All the lights are off in the house except for one. That's the oil lamp out in the foyer. It presents a picture of prayerfulness and the presence of God. Two security guards are outside to protect the Metropolitan's life in case of any attack from extremists of one kind or another. Other than that, it is incredibly quiet. I turn on a low-wattage side lamp beside my bed. It makes the darkness feel soft. My leather, three-ring file sits nearby, reminding me of all the many matters to which I must soon attend. They include several trips that are already planned to dozens of dioceses in various parts of Asia. And then there's another College of Bishops* just around the corner.

Sleep escapes me and is replaced by such a sense of foreboding as I have never known before. Once again, my heart begins to pound, like a warning drum. The thunderstorm of accusations returns in full force, flooding my mind with the charges against the ministry, my integrity, our passion for missions and our sincerity for the Lord. My whole world feels shaken to the core. In response I attempt to pray. I clutch the small, wooden holding cross I keep near my bed and begin asking God

---

* A *College of Bishops* is an official gathering of bishops for a time of prayer and making decisions.

to help me. I wonder if there are demons present that I need to cast out.

If you are wondering, *What on earth happened to him that he is facing such onslaught and crisis?* please bear with me and read on. In chapter 2, I explain why we were cast into such chaos of grief and pain.

As the leader of one of the largest missions in the world, I was always radically committed to keeping my conscience void of any offense toward man and God, with my one and only passion being for my Lord and His Holy Church. But I am now in despair. I had no warning of the magnitude of chaos that would assault me and which now threatened to consume my mind.

I do not know if this experience of mine is the kind of emotional trauma Job of old faced.[4] Everything had been going so well with him and his family. His integrity and reputation were impeccable—he feared God in all his ways.

Even the Lord Almighty testified about Job as "a blameless and upright man, one who fears God and shuns evil."[5] But all of a sudden, without any warning, his world was turned upside down. His wealth vanished, all his children died, his best friends turned against him with harsh accusations, and a community that had respected him began to mock him. Finally, his own wife advised him to "curse God and die"[6] to end his suffering. And would you believe, on top of all this, his fragile body was stricken with awful sores, blood and pus oozing out of these boils.[7]

What do you do when life casts you into confusion? Nothing makes sense. Everything spins out of control. You have no control over what is happening to you. It seems even the foundation you stood on is sucked into this terrible black hole. And your loudest scream is heard by no rescuer.

Is this what King David meant when he said, "My heart is severely pained within me, and the terrors of death have fallen upon me. Fearfulness and trembling have come upon me, and horror has overwhelmed me" (Psalm 55:4–5)? Is this the kind of disappointment that prompted the prophet Elijah to want to die?[8]

I toss and turn in my bed in the semi-dark room. I can't focus. I can't think straight. I wonder if I am going to have a mental breakdown. I know even godly people, like Dr. E. Stanley Jones (1884–1973), who spent much of his time as a missionary in India,[9] and others, were reported to have had mental breakdowns. St. Teresa of Calcutta said, "As far as I am concerned, the greatest suffering is to feel alone, unwanted, unloved."[10] That's where I feel I am—all "alone into the alone."[11]

I just want to give up and have this nightmare end. This is what often happens when someone is in chaos.

Possibly this is what King Solomon writes about in Ecclesiastes 1:2–11, where he mentions that all of life is nothing but chasing the wind. He asks himself, "What is even the point of living?"

✝ ✝ ✝

The nearest I had ever come to such feelings before was back in 1974, just a few weeks after I went to the USA for my college education. My father, who was 74, passed away without any warning. From our tiny village, Niranam, my family tried to call me on the telephone from their trunk line system* for a whole week. My mother and brothers sat in the living room waiting for my return call, but it never came. In the end, they sent me a telegram that simply read, "Father passed away," with the date and time. I was all alone in a strange land, no family, relatives or friends. I remember going out and sitting under a big tree where I cried and cried for so long.

---

* A *trunk line* is a system of calling involving one or more lines and telephone exchanges.

In the movie *Before and After*,[12] a young girl reminisces about the time her teenage brother was accused of murder. In one scene she says, "Your whole life can change in a second, and you never know when it's coming. Before, you think you know what kind of world this is. And after, everything is different for you. Not bad maybe, not always, but different . . . forever. I didn't even know there could be such a thing as *after*. I didn't know that for us, *before* was already over."

The turmoil that followed that moment in time for the girl threatened to destroy her entire family. Life never returned to what it once was for them. The "after" sucked her into the complex arena of rumors, lies, betrayal, distress, alienation and despair. Now in this dark night, I ask myself whether my life, family, ministry or church will ever be the same again.

I have dealt with endless complicated issues in my 50 years of serving God, and most of them while I was in some form of leadership role. I could handle them. But this is not just *complicated*; it is *complex;* it is a fabrication, and I cannot see where it is leading. It is like a hurricane or tsunami that hits with inadequate warning. My well-trained, logical mind struggles to find some reason for this crisis, but I can find nothing

I have done, no wrong that merits this frustration, grief and fear. Please don't misunderstand me, I don't mean to imply that I have not *failed* in my life; I have more times than I can even count.[13] But to my best knowledge, I had *not* committed the many acts that were being alleged against me now.

Finally, I give up. It is getting late. I push the button on my Timex wristwatch, and it lights up, telling me it is two in the morning.

I lay awake, overcome with panic and fear. I pick up one of the books I had been reading, by C.S. Lewis, and the words I read bring some comfort to my troubled heart, which had begun to hurt even more with doubts about God Himself.

C.S. Lewis writes, "Go to Him when your need is desperate, when all other help is vain, and what do you find? A door slammed in your face, and a sound of bolting and double bolting on the inside. After that, silence. . . . The conclusion I dread is not 'So there's no God after all,' but 'So this is what God's really like. Deceive yourself no longer.' "[14]

I think to myself, *I can't believe C.S. Lewis went through this same valley of grief and doubts in which I now find myself.*

I am so exhausted, but I still can't sleep! I think to myself, *I may be losing my mind.* Then suddenly a soft and unnerving voice is heard, as though someone is whispering in my ear, "Kill yourself. There is no other way out. That will end your terrible pain." The voice becomes increasingly strong inside my head. Fear chokes me. I can hardly breathe.

My thoughts now turn to how I might commit this act. I look at the ceiling fan that is some 15 feet above me, and it is as though some foreign personality is guiding my actions: "Take that piece of cloth over there, tie the knot; you can quickly end it all by hanging yourself. It's not that hard. There's no one here. You can do it."

Self-pity begins to take over. I think to myself, *I have given my all to God and the Holy Church. Why is this happening to me?*

Now I am past 65 years of age and feel all alone. I break out in cold sweat and sit up in my bed to pray again. I repeat a simple prayer known as the Jesus Prayer over and over, just as countless believers since the early years of the Church have done: "Lord Jesus Christ, Son of God, have mercy on me, a sinner."[15] Physically reminding myself I belong to Christ, I make the sign of the cross—an action I've practiced for the last several years.

Despite my counter-efforts, I feel like my room is full of dark figures—demons attacking my mind. Never before have I experienced anything like this. I have cast out demons, seen the blind receive their sight, and witnessed scores of people set free from satanic bondage. I have studied demonology, read the early Church's writings on Satan and his works and how to deal with such attacks. I have even written books on spiritual warfare. But believe me, I have never before been in a personal encounter like this with evil forces seeking my very life.

Like a movie in my mind, I can see my dead body being carried down to the predetermined burial place for the Metropolitan. The multitude gathering for the funeral includes all our bishops, clergy and missionaries.

I did not know that silence could be so real, almost more real than matter. I have helped so many all over the world, but now I feel as though God has abandoned me.

My door is shut and locked, and I am walled in. I look up and all I can see is the fan, which is my means of ending this terrible pain and grief. As C.S. Lewis once wrote, "No one ever told me that grief felt so like fear."[16]

✠ ✠ ✠

Miracle!

Suddenly, as if out of nowhere, my room seems to light up. My fears and anxiety, like thick-piled snow, start to melt away. As I come to my senses, I am so ashamed and guilty for allowing myself to forget who I am in Christ and what I represent. Everything changes. Maybe someone was praying for me. It feels just like when, in *The Chronicles of Narnia,*[17] the lion, Aslan, (who represents Christ) is once again on the move after a long period of silence and winter. What looked like eternal snow is quickly melting away all through the land of Narnia. The trees and birds and wildlife are all coming back. And I can almost feel this new life. Thanks to Him, I am still alive!

✠ ✠ ✠

I apologize for writing so long about the chaos and grief I had to endure. That awful night in India, I was tempted to take my life. But the trouble had been building for the last few years on the other side of the globe in East Texas where the American headquarters for GFA World is located.

Just like the St. Thomas Community in India, there is a beautiful community in America as well!

It is situated on some 700 acres of land just an hour away from the city of Dallas, Texas. We moved there in August 2014 when the cost of living on the outskirts of Dallas (our previous headquarters location) rose too high. Our move to this campus in East Texas would save the ministry millions in overhead expenses, meaning even more funds could be sent to the field.

This campus, too, features a beautiful church where our people gather for prayer and worshiping God. St. Peter's Believers Eastern Church is the center of our community life.

I was there when I first discovered that a handful of people were determined to destroy us and this good work the Lord has raised up. It was there that the rumors began, which prompted the writing of that magazine article, and where a lawsuit was eventually filed against us. The rumormongers accused some of our leaders, including me, of fraud and embezzlement. They accused us of being a cult. I initially laughed this off, saying to myself that we had nothing to worry about because the accusations were so absurd. But soon I realized that people were beginning to believe these accusations and that the assault against us was taking root. It felt like a Lucifer-led attack.

Honestly, I never dreamed our ministry and family would face accusations such as those that were made in the lawsuit. Throughout our existence, our heart and our passion have always been to bring Christ's love to a broken and hurting world. We did not look for personal gain. Above all, we sought to honor the Lord in our personal lives, in the way we serve, and by maintaining our integrity.

It has been our practice every year to evaluate our ministry and undergo an independent audit. In 2015, our governing board received a confidential letter from a financial standards association we were part of, and of which we were a charter member, pointing out that our accounting practices needed to better conform to the requirements set by that association. Despite the unique challenges our organization faces by supporting ministry in certain parts of the world, we immediately set out to implement changes based off their letter and even hired a new auditing firm to help us.

One of the things we were criticized for was the cash reserves we kept on the field, which should be considered a best practice for all ministries serving in a volatile environment. This was done as an act of good stewardship, to be sure we had funds to care for the thousands of children in our Bridge of Hope centers, along with so many other ministries we are responsible for. In fact, this measure we took is the only reason we were able to survive on the field during these years of struggle and trial.

Unfortunately, the confidential letter was sent by someone we trusted to a number of people, including a blogger, and its contents were put on social media to damage us. Around the same time, a former staff member sent out a negative letter about us to many of our donors.

We quickly learned the eye-opening lesson that social media, which can be an incredible tool for good, can also be used as a horrible weapon of destruction— when coupled with the power of gossip and slander—to make false accusations go viral and destroy the reputation of others. Too often we hear stories of these rogue actions destroying the life of a godly pastor, church or organization at little cost to the accuser.

Soon after this chaos began, we lost staff members and several thousand supporters. Together with our leadership team, we prayed and tried to reconcile with those who had distanced themselves as a result of the false allegations. Unfortunately, we soon learned that a lawsuit had been filed, which eventually turned into a class action case that enlisted all our supporters as plaintiffs. For that reason, we were severely limited in what we could freely say publicly, and so the explanation of our side of the story was mostly limited to the filings in the lawsuit during those years.

In the meantime, we submitted to the organizational and personal financial investigations under the due process of the court. We even went one step further and retained one of the top four internationally renowned accounting firms to conduct an objective analysis of the flow of GFA World's funds to the field. The field leaders also hired the same top accounting firm's counterpart to review all the funds from overseas and how they had been used. This took an enormous amount of time and money. The audit on the field side alone took a year to complete and cost roughly $1 million USD (which was paid for by the church on the field). In the end, it was concluded that *all* the money given had indeed made it to the field—a conclusion we knew to be true from the very beginning. There was *no* evidence of missing funds or self-enrichment as the accusations against us claimed.

After three years of enormous financial and personal strain to sustain the ministry and pay large legal fees, the court asked us to attempt to settle. Several senior Christian leaders strongly advised us to take this road. Our board members met and decided, after careful consideration, to accept the settlement, knowing that if the lawsuit continued for another two to three years, nothing would be left of the ministry's resources or reputation.

For me, it was an agonizing struggle to know we would have to pay money that could have been used to help thousands of abandoned widows and children living on the streets. Yet to save the ministry, we had to take this difficult step, trusting the Lord to lift us up once more.

This period of being accused and investigated as a fraud and deserted by close friends was probably the most difficult and loneliest time of my life. I can't tell you how many times I nearly gave up. At times, I had no hope left that the ministry could survive the assault. But we had much to learn through all these difficulties, and the Lord was gracious to see us through. He sustained us through the faithful friends who believed in us and prayed for us.

What blessed me most throughout this long and painful journey was that, even though we suffered much heartache and financial strain, the Lord enabled us to sustain the work being done in some 16 nations. I was amazed to see how the Lord continued to move and work through us, despite the trials we were enduring. For example, in 2018, just one year during that time:

- 289,753 women received free health care training.
- 61,800 illiterate women learned to read and write through our literacy classes.
- 1,132 medical camps were conducted in needy communities, which helped care for tens of thousands of people.
- 4,712 clean water wells (Jesus Wells) were drilled and 11,451 BioSand water filters were installed in communities that needed clean water.
- 25,000 needy individuals and families received warm blankets.
- Hundreds of thousands of poor people were helped through income-generating gifts.
- More than 70,000 children were helped to find hope for a better future through Gospel for Asia's Bridge of Hope Program. (Please read my book *No Longer a Slumdog*[18] to get a full picture of this amazing part of our ministry to the poorest of the poor in numerous needy nations.)
- By God's grace and mercy, as I write this, we now have more than 12,000 well-established

local congregations in 16 nations, and we continue to reach out to new regions with the love of Christ. Another 3,000 fellowships gather even now to grow deeper in their walks with the Lord, and we believe they too will soon turn into established churches.

- More than 2,500 young adults have committed their lives to serve the Lord in our dozens of seminaries throughout the world's neediest nations. Preparations are also underway to expand our medical services to African nations and to set up seminaries on that continent to train the younger generation to serve the Lord.

This is for the year 2018, but this is not an exception. For more than 40 years, we have seen results similar to these of what the Lord has done.

✝ ✝ ✝

We give no offense in anything, that our ministry may not be blamed. But in all things we commend ourselves as ministers of God: in much patience, in tribulations, in needs, in distresses, in stripes, in imprisonments, in tumults, in labors, in sleeplessness, in fastings; by purity, by knowledge, by longsuffering, by kindness, by the Holy Spirit, by sincere love, by the word of truth, by the power of God, by the armor of righteousness on the right hand and on the left, by honor and dishonor, by evil report and good report; as deceivers, and yet true; as unknown, and yet well known; as dying, and behold we live; as chastened, and yet not killed; as sorrowful, yet always rejoicing; as poor, yet making many rich; as having nothing, and yet possessing all things (2 Corinthians 6:3–10).

I've read Apostle Paul's words again and again. I've imagined the endless pain, the abuse, the grief, the accusations, the close-to-breakdown experiences, the imprisonment, and yes, the betrayals by friends and co-workers, and I've often thought to myself, *Apparently this is the delivery charge I also have been given to pay, by my suffering and embracing death to myself, to be able to take Christ to the ends of the earth. Well, so be it, Lord.*

How wonderful that now I can open the old, wooden door of my home *(aramana)* in India and see the sun coming up. The night *is* gone. I say to myself, *How foolish I was to wallow in self-pity. I acted as a senseless animal, like the godly man in the psalms.*[19] The expanse of the Kingdom is often bloody. The enemy's bullets are not blanks! All too often they are real. So are Satan and his millions of demons real! But without being willing to do battle and even die if necessary, we will never fulfill the call of God. He wishes for the world He created for us to be reconciled with the Holy Trinity. But, thank God, no one can kill a man who, for all practical purposes, is already dead to himself!

There is a saying in my native language, "The massive, wooden log is a heavy burden for the elephant, and the same is true for the ant that carries a grain of rice." As you read the account of this struggling pilgrim, I am certain you, too, have gone through, or are even now going through, your own Gethsemane. Please believe me, the sun *will* rise. Hold on. Let us not forget God's unchanging promise, "I will never leave you nor forsake you" (Hebrews 13:5). You are *never* alone. I can't imagine how I would have survived if it were not for the prayers of God's people.

The only response when we are plunged into chaos is to let go, let it be, and abandon our life completely into His hands.

✝ ✝ ✝

When we're cast into chaos and faced with suffering, our whole being longs for a way out, but often we find it is only the beginning of a journey through the forest fire of grief where we feel God is suddenly silent.

Yet, we want to know the *why* of this pain, what is the cause? In the next chapter we will talk about the reason for our crisis and pain.

The question remains forever without a satisfying answer: *Why do the righteous suffer?* Job must have asked that a thousand times. Perhaps some things are destined to remain a mystery!

But we know that God works *all* things together for our good[20]—all bad things and all good things. God is in control of *all* that we face in life, and we must trust Him in the bad, as well as the good.

The choice not to give up is *mine*. It is also *yours*.

∽

CHAPTER TWO

DEEP IN THE FOREST FIRE

God has not ceased to love us even though we have offended Him very much. Thus the Lord is right in wanting all to pardon the wrongs done to them.
— St. Teresa of Avila[1]

My day began at 2:45 a.m., well before dawn. Like I'd done so often, I got up, being careful to quietly climb out of bed so I wouldn't wake Gisela from her deep sleep. I was as quiet as I could be on my way out of the bedroom, opening the door to my study gingerly. This time it didn't work! I was caught.

"Why are you not sleeping?" Gisela said. "Where are you going?"

I said, "Try to go back to sleep. I need to work on this book. The deadline is close!"

A few hours pass as I sit alone, thinking, meditating and praying about this chapter I would work on next.

Now it is 8:10 in the morning. As I was about to start writing, my wife walked into my study, laughing. I asked her what had happened.

She responded, "Oh, I was in the kitchen, and a fairy tale that my grandmother told me when I was a little girl came to mind, and it made me laugh." She must have heard that story 60 years ago, and she still remembered it. Of course, I asked her to tell me the fairy tale. She did, and I laughed too!

The fairy tale was about this bad wolf that tried to trick little lambs, pretending to be their mother so he could eat them. The not so funny parts of the story were the plotting, conspiracy and sinister intentions of the bad wolf and his friends as they schemed how to kill and eat the mother sheep and her seven little kids.

But the story ends triumphantly with the mother sheep and her children surviving the bad wolf, and they celebrate by dancing for the sheer joy of still being alive!

I've thought about that story of the bad wolf and the helpless mother sheep with her kids since then, and I realized that it struck a chord because it reflects the sense of helplessness we felt over these last few years of dealing with the crisis in which we'd found ourselves. Because of my faith in the mercy of God, I had to choose to believe all would turn out for good in accordance with Romans 8:28–29.

For us, the mother sheep represented the Almighty God, for we are like a bunch of helpless little lambs. Jesus sent us out into the "enemy-occupied territory,"[2] as C.S. Lewis coined it, as sheep among wolves. The wolf represented the cleverness, plotting and scheming that were going on against us.

On our own, we can never be a match for wolves. Our only hope is the Great Shepherd who will protect us. Even when He is unseen and silent, and He often is, I must choose to see Him, hear Him even when my human ears are dead, serve Him even when all my emotions are empty and dry. Faith is the only ray of hope that shines through the pitch-dark circumstances around us. The sun is still shining brightly in the sky, and I must look through the fog and the thick clouds, face the brightness above, and see the Son though I cannot see!

✝ ✝ ✝

Conspiracy. Over the past few decades, the meaning of that word seems to have shifted to something imaginary or cooked up. An example would be, some people say the moon landing was a conspiracy, a created hoax— "It never happened."

What I have in mind when I use the word is a *real* plot. It's when real, concrete, secret plans are put together to destroy a person, a family, a movement or even a nation. Great men and great nations have fallen because those with ill intentions conspired against them, made plans and put them into motion, executing campaigns of publicity as well as outright violence to destroy what they hate. Such conspiracies have existed as far back in history as we can remember. Conspiracies have existed as long as there have existed people and organizations that have mustered enough hatred to focus on others, as far back as when Caesar was conspired against, to the extent that even his closest confidante raised the knife against him.

So, when I write the word *conspiracy,* I am using it in its true sense. I am stating that around the turn of the century, a tangible plan was hatched by a religious extremist group in Southeast Asia that, in time, would negatively affect me, our U.S. organization (GFA World), and our Believers Eastern Church in numerous countries of Asia. Those involved were committed to shutting down all Christian organizations that had any direct or indirect influence in changing the traditional way of life in the nations where we served. Restated, their goal was to preserve what they saw as their national *culture* and not allow overseas influences to again gain control over their nation. This had happened during India's long and difficult 200 years of colonial rule.

This group was apparently convinced that religion was a new weapon in this ongoing battle to change their nations, and ultimately destroy their culture as they knew it. As of today, many Western-based organizations have already been forced to leave some of these countries for this very reason. The word *conversion* to the Western Church means spiritual transformation, but for these once-colonized nations ruled by the British, they see converting to Christianity as a new way for Western nations to control their countries, and the weapons they feel Westerners use are *religion* and *war*. These once-colonized countries call it "neo-colonialism!"

A few years ago, a major, influential book was published by a highly educated man who I believe is part of this conspiracy movement. This book was dedicated to attacking all forms of Christian work, even those just helping the poor and needy in the name of Christ. The author writes a massive amount of lies about *me* in several pages in his book. In one place he writes that I am the agent of Western countries, and I am appointed and paid to proselytize Indians to Christianity. The fact is, I have never met any government officials or anyone representing them. The truth is, *I* don't like the word *conversion* because it implies forcing people to change their culture and faith by external force or with the persuasion of monetary benefits of some kind. Faith is the personal choice and freedom for people to believe what they believe or don't believe. God never forces anyone to believe in Him either.

Later on, we discovered that even before any of the accusations arose from American sources, these people on the other side of the globe had already begun discussions on how to marginalize and stop the work being done through our movement, where we share the love of Christ in *deed* and *word*.

When I initially heard some of the negative talk describing our work as converting people to Christianity and making them give up their native culture, I felt it was ludicrous. At the same time, some of the churches that had been supporting us in the West began to discontinue their contributions because they were convinced we were becoming too "Eastern" in our ministry's look and approach. (As the leader of this work, I sometimes felt like I couldn't win for losing!)

All I wanted (and still want) was to share the "love of Christ,"[3] as was often said by St. Teresa of Calcutta (commonly known as Mother Teresa), in the best way possible to help the poor and suffering, and to bring new life and goodness to wherever it was most needed. I had no agenda to make native people become Western. It's the opposite of who I am and what I believe in. So initially, I gave such criticisms little credence.

But I must confess that I grossly underestimated these conspirators' resolve and determination. And they were willing, if not eager, to use their influence and power to, if possible, dismantle GFA World in the U.S. and the other supporting offices around the world. From what I now understand, their strategy was to destroy our financial base. Without funds from the West, this group believed our work on the Asian subcontinent would soon be over.

✛ ✛ ✛

As Bible readers know, the Scriptures are full of conspiratorial stories. The Egyptian Pharaoh plotted to kill all the Jewish male children in his land.[4] Mighty Samson's demise was brought about by certain Philistines conspiring with Delilah.[5] Wicked Queen Jezebel, along with the royal family, plotted the death of the prophet Elijah.[6] Jealous Haman conspired to annihilate all the Jews in the giant kingdom of Persia, a plot that was foiled by the young and beautiful Queen Esther.[7] There are many more examples, and, of course, the most dastardly of all conspiracies was Judas's collusion with the religious leaders to betray the Son of God.[8]

I remind myself regularly that it is a mistake to think that if we live our lives righteously, we will be spared such chicanery. Not only is there nothing in the Bible to suggest this, its pages reveal quite the opposite. Remember this passage St. Paul writes to the believers at Corinth: "To the present hour we both hunger and thirst, and we are poorly clothed, and beaten, and homeless. And we labor, working with our own hands. Being reviled, we bless; being persecuted, we endure; being defamed, we entreat. We have been made as the filth of the world, the offscouring of all things until now" (1 Corinthians 4:11–13).

In the last 40 years, GFA has done a lot of good work, but among all the heartwarming stories of positivity, alongside the success stories of every person helped and every soul touched, there are also stories of opposition, imprisonment and even the killing of God's servants. One of our church leaders in Nepal was unjustly imprisoned and separated from his wife and children for nine long years after false witnesses testified against him and accused him of murder. Yet even in such terrible circumstances, he continued his ministry from within the prison, and many inmates came to grasp the love of the Lord Jesus through his faithfulness. Later in this book I will tell you about a missionary called Joseph, who was martyred for his faith.

Even I have received death threats. So far, my life has been spared. But I take these advance warnings seriously, as much as I am able.

The attacks we've faced from this group of conspirators over the years have been relentless. They have come through entire books written against us, work-for-hire reporters who write negative articles, letters written to governments in Asia to stir up trouble, bloggers willing to spread their agenda, and more.

Were you aware that false stories spread about *six* times faster on social media than true ones do?[9] Far too many fake rumors have been spread through social media. This is a horrible trend that is happening more and more that I believe is doing great harm to humanity and the work of God.

In their book *LikeWar: The Weaponization of Social Media,* Singer and Brooking's analysis paints an ominous picture of the scope of the internet in propagating false news on huge, almost unimaginable scales:

Yet, even as social media users are torn from a shared reality into a reality-distorting bubble, they rarely want for company. With a few keystrokes, the internet can connect like-minded people over vast distances and even bridge language barriers. Whether the cause is dangerous (support for a terrorist group), mundane (support for a political party), or inane (belief that the earth is flat), social media guarantees that you can find others who share your views. Even more, you will be steered to them by the platforms' own algorithms. As groups grow, it becomes possible for even the most far-flung of causes to coordinate and organize, to gain visibility and find new recruits.[10]

This dichotomy between reality and social media reality can, of course, be used by those intent on destroying ministries, altruistic outreaches or reputations.

The *LikeWar* authors go on to say:

In numerous studies, across numerous countries, involving millions of people, researchers have discovered a cardinal rule that explains how information disseminates across the internet, as well as how it shapes our politics, media, and wars. The best predicator is not accuracy or even content; it is the number of friends who share the content first.

They are more likely to believe what it says—and then to share it with others who, in turn, will believe what *they* say. It is all about us, or rather our love of ourselves and people like us. This phenomenon is called "homophily," meaning "love of the same."[11]

Christianity excels at teaching us to practice what a friend I know calls "the positive opposite." Most of these practices find their genesis in Christ's teachings. The primary example of this is, "Bless those who persecute you; bless and do not curse."[12]

Most of us, when we face some sort of *concerted* conspiracy of criticism, basically plead for the ability to survive it. It takes a while to remember to pray for our persecutors.

✛ ✛ ✛

As I referenced already in the first chapter, one of the main ways we were defamed was regarding our financial integrity. It was only later we learned about religious fundamentalists who were behind the scenes and directing such false claims and accusations. This was done to accomplish their overall goal of destroying us.

The most shocking thing about the lawsuit was the absurdity of the claims against us. The claims were completely at odds with who we are or how we have conducted ourselves in these four decades of serving our Lord and His Holy Church among some of the poorest and neediest people in the world.

We have been focused, like a laser beam, on only one thought and passion: to know our Lord intimately and to go to the ends of the earth to see that the untold multitudes could find hope in Christ—in His death, burial and resurrection.

Since the start of the ministry, I have been consumed with this singular question: *How can we find more resources to share the love of God with more people in the shortest amount of time possible?* I am constantly aware of what little time we have left to bring hope to these people in need. What I did not consider, however, nor fully understand, was the significant growth of our ministry from year to year. Before we knew it, we had become one of the largest mission movements in the world.

With thousands of workers serving in numerous nations, and a massive budget needed to do the work, I could only think about how to grow faster before it was too late. And all along our opposition continued plotting, targeting us.

In the middle of everything, I couldn't see the bigger picture. I couldn't see the powers of darkness at work, or God's hand trying to teach me that I can't depend on anything but Him alone. I had yet to learn about the fellowship of His suffering that I had never quite entered into before. More than once I wondered where God was in all that was taking place.

✠ ✠ ✠

Let me tell you a story, a real story.

When I was studying in the 5th grade, in my tiny village in South India, I had to walk three kilometers to school with other students. The winding path we walked was the same every day. Once I saw a coin that someone had lost lying on the path. I picked it up. The coin's value was about 10 cents in U.S. money. But for me at the time, it was like finding $100! It would buy a lot of candy! When I reached home, I told my father that I had found this coin on the road. Could I buy sweets with it?

He was silent for a minute. Then asked me, "Son, whose money is this?"

"I don't know."

"Then it must belong to someone else, right? For the next 30 days, ask all your friends and others if any of them lost a coin. If no one claims it, then after 30 days you can use it to buy candies."

I found no one who claimed the exact amount of that coin, so I happily bought myself some peanut candy!

For some reason I have never forgotten that incident. To this day, it is said that if ever one man lived in my village who never lied, it was my father. He was the most honest individual I have ever known.

I grew up in a home like that. I am not saying we were perfect people. I have family members who did not live as my father did. But I always wanted to be like him. So, when these financial allegations were first launched against me, they seemed divorced from reality. It truly didn't occur to me that they would be taken seriously.

But not everyone saw them that way.

✝ ✝ ✝

I have always known that the individuals who support GFA World are people who are careful with their money. It pains me deeply to imagine the shock they must have experienced when we were attacked deliberately and mercilessly with absolute lies that were made to appear as the truth. It hurts me more when I think about how many must have thought, "Here goes another fake Christian leader and his work!"

I have cried thinking about the innocent people who trusted us and were hurt by the lies of the devil about us. One of my reasons for writing this book is my hope that if you are one who was hurt in this way, you will now know the rest of the story and find joy in the privilege the Lord gave you in being a part of accomplishing His will through our ministry.

In the span of only a few months, we began rapidly losing sponsors of field workers and sponsors of children we were helping—some 70,000 children in 520 centers scattered about in many Asian nations. Organizationally, our income streams narrowed and narrowed until we were drying up. I got frightened.

Then came the many requirements of the lawsuit. How could we be expected to provide proof of millions and millions of blankets produced and distributed? The plaintiffs wanted a record of each and every individual who had been given a blanket, a chicken, a goat, etc. Even if we were able to do it, it would take years to compile all that information from around the many remote locations where we serve (and we were only given months). Despite the enormous difficulty of the requests, we worked night and day, doing all we could to provide the information being asked of us.

It is worth noting that in all the countries we serve, records are maintained of all funds received and spent. Yearly independent audits are also done. Even so, with the whole process, coupled with the accusations and the pressure felt by whole the ministry, I was deeply distressed. Yet as I look back, I can see the Lord working.

We submitted to so many questions and so many requests under the due process of the court. I'm grateful that in the end, the *final* court document concluded that both parties mutually stipulate that all donations designated for use in the field were ultimately sent to the field.

One unique blessing GFA has experienced over the past years of our mission is how many of our donors and sponsors have actually traveled to the field nations where we serve—people who are sponsors of children in our centers and of our field workers serving the Lord. These supporters are people who have given financially to build local churches, buy bicycles, animals and even boats to reach island dwellings. Some contributed to help build our seminary campuses and dozens of other projects. Among all those who have traveled to the field to see the results of their generosity, we have never had even one sponsor say, "We gave money for this child, or to build a church in that place, but when we went to that country to see the church or meet the child we support, we could not find them there."

Once, a donor who had given a huge one-time gift of 3.5 million U.S. dollars to establish a seminary with a large campus came with me to visit one of the South Asian nations where we have a presence. This subject came up in our conversation. So I said to him, "This place where we are, this is the land and the buildings that were furnished with your most generous gift." This place is now a 34-acre campus with our seminary, school and church—a place where all God's people now gather for conferences, education and worship.

For over three years, we carried this enormous burden to sustain the ministry in the midst of the court case. It was a dark night that seemed to never end, and without faith it would have felt hopeless. In my case, very few of my friends even called to ask what was happening or how they could help. I felt more alone and abandoned than I ever had before in my life.

✝ ✝ ✝

These times were some of the darkest and most painful I have ever known. I will forever be grateful to all who walked alongside us during that time and for their steadfastness, prayers and encouragement.

I am now aware that, all around the world, friends and concerned individuals were praying behind the scenes, and even fasting on our behalf and for the sake of the ministry, for us to be able to continue what the

Lord had begun. Maybe it was *you* who prayed for me on that awful night I spent in my bedroom in India.

I would be remiss not to write that in some unexpected way, I believe this journey I have been on, my longest journey to date, has made me a better servant of the Lord and of His Church. I did not think I would eventually come to feel this way during those days when I walked through that valley of darkness, through that raging forest fire.

When I look back now, more and more of the puzzle pieces start to fit into place. I realize that beneath the surface, there was so much more to everything we went through than the limited knowledge we had at first. We now know that so much of what we went through was schemed and planned for years, by extremists seeking to destroy us.

To them, we had surfaced as possibly the greatest threat to people who had never before heard about Christ. Through us, people had the opportunity to see things differently, to experience freedom through the love of the Father. For them, the focus was not on people hearing about Christ's love, but on the fear that people in these nations would lose their loyalty to their own nations.

Today, Christians are being turned away from their love for each other and for the Great Commission to a self-love that proclaims, "Better him than me," or "Serves him right." Some have turned into mob-like actors, ready to cast stones even at church leaders.

When did God call us to attack fellow Christians? He never has. That's the Devil's role. Can we not come alongside our brothers and sisters when they are limping and struggling and help them stand again? Even if they have done wrong, can we not help ensure that they are restored?[13] We are never called to destroy them.

The great reality of the Christian message is not that people fail, not that they are flawed, but that there is redemption, reconciliation and reclamation available in the Cross of Jesus Christ. Instead of criticism, we should be praying for resurrection of the human spirit that has been broken by sin (even when the brokenness is caused by those who disappoint and disillusion us). Regeneration is one of the ongoing triumphant messages of Christianity.

I have walked through this minefield—the abuse was aimed at me. I was the target. But sadly, I don't believe this is a story exclusive to me and the ministry of GFA. I am convinced that in the days ahead, many other ministries will face this same onslaught. The journey I've been writing about is not just about us. We are only a guinea pig, a test case, so the enemy sees how far he can go. But it will not always be someone else who is the object of attack. Persecution, malicious gossip, and the collusion of evil to destroy can even happen to *you*. When you walk through the forest fire of grief and pain, though, you will see the invisible One and He will see you through.

✛ ✛ ✛

We have read of Daniel and his friends thrown into the fiery furnace—which was heated seven times hotter than usual.[14] The blue flame should have turned them into a pinch of ashes in seconds. Yet they were alive, able to walk in it. Most awe-inspiring of all was that a fourth figure (the invisible One) joined them in the blue flame. He made Himself visible to the onlookers from behind their protective wall.

Just like Christ was with Daniel and his friends, He is with us, too. Though our journeys are of a different kind, they are meant for us to learn how to become more like Him so we may have the inner strength to persevere in our suffering. That is what we will talk about in the next chapter.

The sun will rise!

CHAPTER THREE

SUFFERING IS
THE WAY OF LIFE

*Do not claim to have acquired virtue unless you
have suffered affliction, for without affliction virtue has not been tested.*

— St. Mark the Ascetic[1]

Someone once wrote in a blog that I drive a vintage
European sports car, which anyone would have
taken to mean I drive a flashy, expensive vehicle. The
truth is, I drive a *1962 VW Bug*. This is the *only* car
I own anywhere in the world. I bought it for $1,800
from a young American girl going to serve as a missionary in Manila, the Philippines. You will like the story.
Let me share it with you.

About 24 years ago, I told my secretary to keep
looking in the daily newspaper for someone with an
old VW Bug for sale.

One day she came to me and said, "I found one, but it is so old you may not like it."

I called the number in the paper, and a young girl answered. I asked her many questions, and she assured me that it still ran. She was asking US $1,600 in the ad.

So, we agreed to meet halfway at a McDonald's, because she lived nearly two hours from us. My wife, Gisela, and I drove to the small town of McKinney, north of Dallas, Texas, and there the young woman was waiting with her faded yellow, 1962 VW Bug.

We exchanged greetings and got acquainted. I asked, "My, this thing is so old, where did you get it from?" She told the long story of how she was given the car. All the parts—everything—even the torn seats in it were original. The paint was peeling off here and there, but there were no dents anywhere. I joked, "You are asking too much for this old car!"

She was quiet for a moment and then said, "Sir, the truth is I kind of need $1,800, but I didn't think I would get that, so I lowered the price to $1,600."

"Why $1,800?"

"You see, I just finished college and I am going with a mission to Manila in the Philippines to serve the poor in the slums there. I have to raise that much money for my trip."

She had no clue who I was. My wife and I looked at each other, smiled and wrote her a check for $1,800. We told her about our own work and blessed her for her willingness to serve the Lord in Asia. I still drive that car today.

Just the other day, I learned that the girl who sold us the car is still serving in the Philippines today! How amazing that the Lord would allow my need for a car to be part of this girl's journey to share Christ's love all the way around the world for so many years.

✛ ✛ ✛

The other day, I was talking to Gisela about this book. I told her, "I am hoping to share a few things about our family in this book—for we seldom talk about our private lives in public." I felt, as St. Paul did in 2 Corinthians, that with all these accusations against us, we needed to reveal something of how we live.

But my wife's eyes were sad. She said, "I don't want to say anything to anyone. Good or bad, all I care about is our walk with Him, and I am happy to suffer in silence for His sake. Why do we need people's approval? Today they say, 'Hosanna' and tomorrow, 'Crucify Him!' What happened to all your followers who clamored for you to be their mentor? Almost all of them have disappeared!"

I was silent. We have now been married for more than 45 years. I knew her response was the result of the deep pain she was going through.

But I am also persuaded, as St. Paul was, that sometimes leaders need to let outsiders in to see their private lives, because for us, the ministry is *not* our job or career, but our very lives.[2]

Years ago, during one of our USA board meetings, some members suggested that a $15-million insurance policy should be taken on out my life. In case I got killed, my family would then be taken care of. I responded that I could not allow it in good conscience, for I am the servant of servants. Thousands of my co-workers didn't know how they might provide for their family from one month to the next.

Another time, the board wanted to increase my salary significantly. They also noted that Gisela worked full-time for the ministry but never took even a postage stamp to send personal letters to her family in Germany.

For years we said to the board, "Our needs are being met, and that is all that is necessary." Until 2006, we were getting US $50,000 a year. After covering our basic needs, all the rest we received went to the Lord's work.

Then during one board meeting, the members decided Gisela and I should not be present when our revised salary was discussed. Again, we told them *not* to increase our pay, for we didn't need more. But eventually I said to myself, "I must submit to their authority and humble myself in obedience to their wishes."[3]

Sure enough, the salary was raised to $70,000 per year plus home allowance. But privately, Gisela and I decided we would still use those funds only to meet our needs, and we would continue to give the rest to the Lord's work.

And I know of organizations that have a yearly budget comparable to that of GFA World USA, where many of their CEOs make from $300,000 up to $1 million as their yearly salary. I am grateful for their contributions to the Body of Christ, but, for us, the way the Lord led is different.

✝ ✝ ✝

When I was vehemently criticized by a blogger for luxurious living, I said to myself, "If only he knew . . . " These accusations against me, my family and this ministry were constant needles poking at me. I would be resolved and at peace, and then I'd wake up in the middle of the night in knots. I knew in my heart who I was and my purpose for living this life, but I still could not seem to put the accusations to rest.

The funny thing is, I don't even receive any royalties from my 275 plus books, though I have been encouraged by agents who assist Christian authors in the USA to personally benefit financially from my books and copyright materials, just as many other authors do. If I had chosen to do so, I could, by now, have millions to my name. To be frank, I also have some sympathy with the reasons why I was attacked. I know that a simple internet search for "rich pastors" or "church leaders" is all it takes to see how there are people who claim to do the work of our Lord who are *millionaires,* living like kings in their own personal kingdoms. So, I understand why it is easy for people to believe that I am also like them, using ministry for personal enrichment.

Scores of such allegations were spread on social media against us. My hands were tied, and inside I suffered as these rumors spread faster than wildfire—as fast as only gossip and fake news can on social media.

But then I understood from the Bible that such criticism was a part of the reality the Apostle Paul had to deal with,[4] and that Jesus Himself even had to endure it.[5] Still, that realization didn't take away my pain and the creeping desire to simply give up and stop fighting!

Here is one thing every follower of Christ must understand sooner or later: You cannot follow close to Jesus without suffering, no matter where you live in the world.[6]

There is no question that suffering in God's work leads us to know Him more intimately. Suffering is the tool God seems to use to remove our dependence on anything other than Him. During this time of chaos and crisis, one of the nicest things that happened is much like in the *Chronicles of Narnia,* when every now and then Aslan, the lion, (a Christ figure) shows up.

I remember it was a night when I had a most vivid dream. By the way, I am *not* one who seeks to interpret every dream I have, but all I could see in this dream was how the night was blacker than black and the clouds were so dark and threatening. Then suddenly, right in the middle of this thick, black cloud, a light began to shine.

It was exactly the shape of a cross. Later, I realized this dream lingered in my mind throughout the day, the vision imprinted in my memory. Immediately, I recalled St. Paul's statements about his longing "that I may know Him and the power of His resurrection, and the fellowship of His sufferings, being conformed to His death, if, by any means, I may attain to the resurrection from the dead" (Philippians 3:10–11).

These thoughts began working in my heart in the following days, and it was like I could breathe again. The road continued to be rough and hard going. But it was a significant turning point through this maze of suffering I was going through.

✝ ✝ ✝

In the Book of Exodus, we read about the miraculous deliverance of the children of Israel from their slavery and suffering in ancient Egypt. They were free! The rejoicing with singing and dancing was heard loud and clear.

Soon after their wonderful experience, they were thirsty while traveling through the desert of Shur.[7] For days they had nothing to drink. Then they came upon a body of water—but it was bitter! Then God showed Moses a piece of wood and told him to throw it into the bitter water. Instantly the waters of Marah became sweet.

This wood is a picture of the cross of our Lord and His suffering and death on the wooden cross. If we allow the cross of Christ—His life of suffering—to enter into our grief, the "bitter waters of Marah" become sweet, and we, too, experience joy in the suffering.

When we go through intense loneliness and pain, we can say, "Lord Jesus, I now understand a little of what You suffered for me." This is a choice we must all make, to relate what we face to our Lord's life, His Cross, death and resurrection.

This is what we read about St. Paul. He chose to suffer and die for his master, Christ. He didn't regard his life on earth as dear to himself. Jesus became more precious to him than his very own life.[8]

Another event we read about in the Book of Acts is when St. Stephen was brutally killed for speaking about Christ. While religious fanatics stoned him to death, he glanced upward and saw the Heavens open and the Lord Jesus standing looking at him! "Lord, forgive them,"[9] he prayed.

What struck me most is that Jesus also stood there, watching what happened. I remember thinking to myself while reading this account, *Why is He not rescuing him? Why does He allow him to be so cruelly stoned to death?*

Read further. Stephen may not have known, but not that far from his broken, bloodied body there was a young man taking all this in—his name was Saul, who later became the Apostle Paul. What a mystery! When I think about all the betrayals and people causing me pain and grief, I realize, *I am serving a God who is not bound by time, space and matter.* I can honestly say I don't hate my tormentors. Not one. I pray for them. I really do. For our God, all time is the present. A wicked man can be a godly saint after some time. And God, who sees him when he is a wicked sinner like Saul, also sees him transformed into the image of His Son. This is the teaching of the early Church fathers, the men who led the Church during the first centuries after Christ's ascension, when persecution and getting killed was a way of life for those who chose to follow Christ.

St. Paul was to become one of the most important individuals in the history of the Church. Think about it: Were the suffering, the pain, and the injustice he witnessed when godly Stephen was martyred worth it in the light of eternity? Was that the means for Saul to first understand the suffering of Christ and for him to also recognize the great love of God?[10] I think so.

✛ ✛ ✛

I remember meeting an evangelist that our Believers Eastern Church sent to a community to minister. He faced a lot of opposition from opposing fanatics. He fasted and prayed, working tirelessly to share the love of Christ with the people in this community. One day, he was roused from sleep by a knock on his door. He opened the door of his small house, and there stood one of the leaders of the group of people who'd been making his life miserable. This man said, "My only son is dying. Something is wrong with him. I had a dream that if I come and ask you, you will pray to your God, and my son will be healed."

Our evangelist didn't know what was going to happen, wondered if it was a trap to kill him. But God gave him the peace and strength to go with the man. With much fear he went with the man and found the little boy lying in bed in very bad shape. Not even knowing what the problem was, he knelt beside him and laid his hand on his forehead and prayed for him in the name of the Lord Jesus Christ: "Lord, please show Yourself merciful and kind and loving to this family and heal this little one." Believe it or not, the man's son was healed instantly, and that was how seven people came to know the Lord and experience His love. The rest of the story is more glorious. But think with me for a moment. This brother could have said, "I'm tired of being here where I am attacked every single day. I can't even buy groceries without an incident. I am rejected and laughed at. I can't take it. Heal your own son." Thank God he instead obeyed the Lord.

There is another story that makes me cry. There was a worker who was trained at seminary for four years. His prayer was that the Lord would send him to a field that was 2,000 miles away from where he was born, and to a people who had never heard of the love of Christ. The Bishop in that area prayed and sent him out to go to this particular group. When he got there, he realized just how difficult this location was. Everything was strange to him: the food, the language and the culture! But he said to himself, "I prayed for God to send me to a people who had never heard His name, and my church sent me with their prayers." So, with determination he continued to pray, fast and work hard to represent Christ to these suffering and needy people.

But, no matter how hard he labored, nothing seemed to happen. All his efforts resulted in more opposition and mockery from some in the community. Eventually he could not even stomach the smell of the food people ate there. Slowly, his prayer changed: "Lord, I know You sent me here. I want to be here, but I can't stay any longer. It's just too difficult. No one seems to hear and understand, and I'm struggling to learn the language. Despite doing everything I can, I am still rejected and despised, and unaccepted."

One day he was prostrate on his mat, weeping in prayer, "Lord, please give me permission to leave this place and go to another where I can do something more." Then suddenly it was as if he could hear the Lord speaking clearly in his heart: "You can go, son. Go wherever you can be comfortable, but I will stay. These people are My people; they need to know Me and that I love them." The words broke him. He wept and pledged his life, saying, "Lord, if nothing happens here, if all I can do is lay down my life, I will do that, I will not leave." He continued living there and learned to eat the food and helped the poor people build their homes, and he became a loving, kind friend in the community. He was able to help build over 100 houses for the homeless in that community. Eventually, he learned the language and customs, and he gained acceptance.

Today there are over 450 local parishes, formed into four dioceses, in that region that gather for the divine liturgy every Sunday to hear God's Word, worship and partake in Holy Communion. They established a seminary in their local diocese. They also started a radio broadcast in the language of the people.

All this happened because someone was willing to give his life. Suffering would not drive him away. This is not an isolated account. There are hundreds of such men and women who live by the teaching of our Lord, just like in the Gospels and the Book of Acts.

To give a more complete picture, I should probably add that in many of the nations where we serve, suffering has often been faced by new believers. In that regard, I think of the words of St. John of Avila: "Christ tells us that if we wish to join Him, we shall travel the way He took. It is surely not right that the Son of God should go His way on the path of shame while the sons of men walk the way of worldly honor."[11]

It was St. Francis of Assisi (1182–1226) who said, "I hope that I so blessed will be that every suffering pleases me."[12]

Suffering, pain, misunderstandings, gossip and the lies people say about us, fears and anguish and grief—this is all part of being in enemy territory. Jesus set an example for us to follow. We read this in Scripture, "For to this you were called, because Christ also suffered for us, leaving us an example, that you should follow His steps" (1 Peter 2:21).

St. Paul says this statement right after saying how he and the others ministering with him are "always carrying about in the body the dying of the Lord Jesus, that the life of Jesus also may be manifested in our body. For we who live are always delivered to death for Jesus' sake, that the life of Jesus also may be manifested in our mortal flesh."[13]

What Apostle Paul was talking about was not about somebody beating him up and shooting him with a weapon to try and kill him. No. He was talking about the daily choice, every minute, of saying "no" to yourself and "yes" to God.

St. Paul would later write in 2 Timothy 2:10, "I endure all things for the sake of the elect, that they also may obtain the salvation which is in Christ Jesus with eternal glory." For 30 years of his life, like a wounded animal dripping blood on the trail his feet followed, he faced unbelievable persecution and suffering and endured all to preach the Good News.[14] Sitting in prison he said, "But I want you to know, brethren, that the things which happened to me have actually turned out for the furtherance of the Gospel" (Philippians 1:12).

That means St. Paul evaluated every event in his life, whether it was eating or drinking, traveling, wearing certain clothes, or who he associated with. He evaluated it all based on how it would contribute to him being able to share the hope of Christ with others. He was so focused that he spent his entire life for one thing: to know the Lord Jesus Christ and make Him known to those who never knew Him, no matter the cost to himself.[15]

✢ ✢ ✢

The Book of Acts chapter four records the persecution that first-generation Christians faced. There we also read of the prayers they offered. They were not for God to remove the suffering, rather their prayers focused on the glory of the Lord Jesus and that they would have the grace to be His bold witnesses.

Then it says, "They were all filled with the Holy Spirit, and they spoke the word of God with boldness."[16] Suffering mustn't make us run away from the precious life of our Lord, but rather become a part of it. We enter into the life of Christ through suffering; we embrace it for His sake.

Scripture says, Jesus "learned obedience from the things he suffered."[17] What is this verse referring to? Not the cross, nails and brutal beating and crucifixion. If that be so, all those who want to follow Christ should look to be crucified as He was! Instead, for His entire life Jesus gave up His own wishes, gave up gladly a million things He could have wished for as a man, only to joyfully say "NO" to Himself in order to do the will of His Father.[18]

He suffered physically, mentally and emotionally throughout His life. Why? He was learning to renounce His will completely for His Father's sake.

✝ ✝ ✝

Let me share a story I heard told many years ago.

An old missionary couple, who had been working in Africa for years, were going back to New York City to retire. They had no pension; their health was broken; they were defeated, discouraged, and afraid. They discovered they were booked on the same ship as President Teddy Roosevelt, on his way back from a hunting expedition.

No one paid much attention to them. They watched the fanfare that accompanied the President's entourage, with passengers trying to catch a glimpse of the great man.

As the ship pulled into the harbor, the old missionary said to his wife, "Something is wrong. Why should we have given our lives in faithful service for God in

Africa all these many years and have no one care a thing about us? Here this man comes back from a hunting trip and everybody makes much over him, but nobody gives two hoots about us."

"Dear, you shouldn't feel that way," his wife said.

"I can't help it; it doesn't seem right."

When the ship docked in New York, a band was waiting to greet the President. The mayor and other dignitaries were there. The papers were full of the President's arrival, but no one noticed this missionary couple. They slipped off the ship and found a cheap apartment and hoped tomorrow they could see what they could do for a living.

That night, the husband's spirit broke. He said, "I can't take this; God is not treating us fairly."

His wife replied, "Why don't you go into the bedroom and tell that to the Lord?"

A short time later he came out from the bedroom, but he looked changed. His wife asked, "Dear, what happened?"

"The Lord settled it with me," he said. "I told him how bitter I was that the President should receive this tremendous homecoming when no one met us as we returned home. And when I finished, it seemed as though the Lord put his hand on my shoulder and simply said, 'But you're not home yet!' "[19]

Like the man in this story, when we encounter suffering in our lives, we should not feel as if we are being treated unfairly or cry to be delivered from it, like I was so often tempted to do. Instead, we pray, "God, give me the strength to stay faithful to You." That is what Jesus said to Peter: "Satan wants to tempt you in order to destroy you, but I have prayed that your faith will not fail."[20] It is through suffering that we learn, like Jesus, how to do the Father's will.

✠ ✠ ✠

Somehow our instincts long for clear answers to questions like, "What's next?" Learning the history of God's dealings with His people, like those in the Old Testament and New Testament, will tell us that "God's ways are beyond and above us."[21] Our focus should be to follow Him. In my case, the trials and agony did not present a straight line of logic. There were many twists and turns through this forest fire, and one of the most important lessons in it for me was that I understood the life and journey of the early Christians, the Apostles and Fathers of the Church, a little better—I learned to know His ways in the classroom of their lives.[22] That's what we will talk about in the next chapter.

Be a learner!

CHAPTER FOUR

MY JOURNEY
TO ANCIENT PATHS

*The way to deeper knowledge of God is through
the lonely valleys of soul poverty and giving up of
all things.*

— A.W. Tozer[1]

"**A**nd that's not the half of it!"

Often that's what people say when the experience they've been describing takes longer to relate than what they had envisioned. That's what I feel even now as I once again explain some of what took place during my period of intense suffering.

There is no doubt in my mind that as you journeyed with me, you felt some of the pain I recounted.

There is one thing I must tell you. I don't think it would have been possible to make it through those days if it wasn't for a journey the Lord started me on about 15 years ago, before the chaos ever began to surface.

In His great mercy, the Lord had seen to it that many years ago I began reading more and more of the accounts of the early Church Fathers who had lived during the first few centuries of the Church. I confess that for most of my life I was rather ignorant of who they were and of the incredible lives they lived. But if I wanted to become acquainted with some fellow travelers who understood what suffering was all about, I would have been hard-pressed to find a better array of commiserating friends!

The Church Fathers are the early and most influential theologians who carefully (and sometimes painfully) articulated the non-negotiable truths of Christian faith through the early centuries of the Holy Church. This includes the writers of the Gospels and the New Testament epistles. Many among the Orthodox Fathers of the Church, also known as Church Fathers, were contemporaries of the apostles, and those the apostles discipled to give leadership to the Holy Church. For example, St. Clement (Bishop Clement of Rome), St. Ignatius of Antioch and Bishop Polycarp of Smyrna.[2]

Their writings, sermons and recorded statements of faith resulted in broad theological consensus and have influenced the development of Christianity through-out the following centuries. That's the kind of impact the cumulative effect of their lives has had.

These men and women knew way more about fiery trials than I ever will. Too many to number were slaughtered because of their faith. The opening years of the Church were tough. Persecution was seldom that far off, and untimely deaths were relatively common-place. Preferring rejection, torture, and even slaughter to renouncing their faith, they served Christ as missionaries, scholars and pilgrims, and their astounding courage and faith changed the world. Reading the literature of this period makes us aware that the church considered martyrdom in a light unknown to us who are moderns: "Christ's martyrs feared neither death nor pain. He triumphed in them who lived in them; and they, who lived not for themselves but for him, found in death itself the way to life."[3]

One of those early Church fathers, St. Ignatius of Antioch, was transported to Rome for execution and wrote that they were not to attempt to rescue him: "Let me be fodder for wild beasts . . . For though alive, it is with a passion for death that I am writing to you . . . There is living water in me, which speaks and says inside me, 'Come to the Father.' . . . I do not want to live any more on a human plane."[4]

Things changed radically after Constantine the Great made Christianity the official religion of the Roman Empire.[5] But that wasn't until the early 300s A.D.

How uplifting it was to discover these old "new friends"—or was it new "old friends"? There were so many of them! And not only was their world more menacing than mine, I found myself intrigued by their intimate and sometimes mystical walks with the Lord. To me, they appeared driven to sacrifice all to live as Christ lived in the world.[6]

I read further about those now referred to historically as the Desert Fathers and Mothers—men and women who so desperately wanted to know God that they left everything and withdrew to the desert to seek Him.[7] They were not one or two individuals, but ever so many, long-gone believers who hungered after God. Their lives truly inspired me.

In my earlier formal studies, I had not been exposed to these incredible Christians. I knew little about Church Fathers such as St. John Chrysostom or St. Antony.[8] People like these wrote with different words and expressions and related testimonies that told of the supernatural in a manner that was often foreign to my spiritual journey. They also heard God speak in ways that were outside of my limited realm. It was all so new and refreshing.

It's fair to write that I was being opened up to a Christianity that was older and more mature and less confined than what I had previously known. I was now privy to much of the marvelous history of the Church after the biblical record ended. God was speaking to me through these giants of the faith. The biblical traditions they lived according to were handed down to the Church leaders that led the Holy Church in the Apostolic faith and traditions, into the centuries that followed the lives of these spiritual titans on earth. God was inspiring me, not just from the Scriptures, but also through the writings of godly people who wanted more than anything else in the world "to know God in experience and escape the corruption of the world," as the Apostle Peter writes in 2 Peter 1:4.[9]

How wonderful, for example, that a decade after this journey began, in my anguish God could now speak to me in a dream, even as He did for some of them.[10] And I didn't have to pick it apart trying to figure it all out. Was the good Lord attempting to minister peace to me, or was it just a silly old dream? These saints didn't try to solve such mysteries. They just wrote what they experienced.

It happened like this: Too often during those three to four years, I fell asleep wishing I wouldn't wake up. But on one such occasion I had a dream of my mother, who had already departed and gone to be with the Lord a few years ago. It was a normal dream, but it was also very real to me. She sat right there on the corner of my bed and talked to me.

"Son, all will be well. This suffering is nothing compared to the joy you will know when you see our Lord."

I replied, "But why is Jesus not helping me? And where is the Father who said the Holy Spirit will come, and He will never forsake me?!" So, on and on I complained and wallowed in my self-pity.

"Mother, I don't know what to do," I continued, and started weeping. That's when I woke up—it took a few seconds for me to realize it had just been a dream, but it was also as though she had really been there.

The next day I kept thinking and thinking about the experience. Then a few weeks later I had another dream just like before. This time I said, "Mother you are dead. I was at your funeral!"

She responded, "No, I'm more alive than when I was with you on earth. Jesus sent me to talk to you. He loves you, and He has heard all your prayers and those of the thousands of others who are interceding on your behalf. He has already answered many prayers, but this trial is to let you become more like Him. Don't give up! Remember what St. Paul said in 2 Corinthians 4:1 (paraphrased), 'Since this ministry is given to us by the Lord, we will not give up and lose heart.'" And then she disappeared again.

Then, would you believe, it happened again—a third dream came, quite similar to the earlier two. (I suppose I'm not such a fast learner!) This time I distinctly recall that I blurted out, "Mother, I'm unhappy with Jesus. In fact, I'm angry at Him."

"Why?" she asked.

"You know, I read so many times in the Bible about King David praying for his enemies to be killed. All I am asking is for God to tell me what I should do! These are terrible people, who are hurting God's Kingdom and wounding me in the process."

"My little son, don't you yet understand that love is the greatest weapon there is in the universe. And in a few years' time, these people you're criticizing could be saints like Paul. Your job is to love them and to do all you can to cooperate with what God is doing."

She got up to leave. I pleaded, "Mother, please don't go. Please stay, I need to ask you more questions."

"Well," she replied. "I may come and see you again, but I am really waiting for the day you will come and join me forever." And that was the last dream I had of her … at least up till now.

I honestly wish I could classify these as normal dreams and be done with it. But they were much more real than I can convey to you with just the words on this page, which seem so inadequate to describe how every sense in me recognized that it was truth.

My mother had a massive influence on my life as she was bringing me up. When I was a little kid being raised in a tiny village in India, she was only 5-foot 1, but her countenance was different from that of any human being I ever saw. It was as if she looked at the same world, we all had in front of our eyes, but she saw a different one from what we saw, as if she saw the Lord's kingdom on earth. I never saw her without hope. I didn't really understand her. I don't think her husband (my father) even understood her. As a young boy, I heard her say so often, *"Whom have I in Heaven but you? And earth has nothing I desire besides you."* Later I would learn that she was quoting Psalm 73:25. She went to be with the Lord at the age of 84. By the way, did you know that in the early Church they used the word *departed* in place of the word *dead?* That's because they saw their fellow believers as still very much alive, but just in another place.

It was much later in my life, as I was studying these early Church writings,[11] that I understood that while living here on earth she was a person who was sharing in the life of God. For her, it wasn't works and pretense; it was a spiritual reality. That was also a reality of the lives of the early Church Fathers and Mothers. They knew God by experience, not only through the theological stance of correct doctrine but in their moment-to-moment real lives.

In these dreams I now believe that God, through my mother, was ministering love and training me for future struggles I will possibly face, including persecution and whatever else may be a part of my pilgrimage ahead.

✣ ✣ ✣

When I was a young man, somebody gave me a book called *The Mystery of Godliness* by Major W. Ian Thomas.[12] I read it numerous times, and I desperately wanted to understand what he was saying. But I never truly grasped the meaning of what he wrote. For me, it was like looking at a beautiful rose with the most alluring scent, but one that was beyond my appreciation.

The book, however, started me thinking thoughts I had never had before about the mystery of godliness. In 1 Timothy 3:16, it reads that the mystery of godliness is that God became flesh. The invisible became visible, and Jesus was the means by which we could see the invisible God. Like I read later in another book: "God became human that we might be made god,"[13] or as some say, "ingodded." C.S. Lewis says:

> The command *Be ye perfect* is not idealistic gas. Nor is it a command to do the impossible. He is going to make us into creatures that can obey that command. He said (in the Bible) that we were 'gods' and He is going to make good His words. If we let Him—for we can prevent Him, if we choose—He will make the feeblest and filthiest of us into a god or goddess, a dazzling, radiant, immortal creature, pulsating all through with such energy and joy and wisdom and love as we cannot now imagine, a bright stainless mirror which reflects back to God perfectly (though, of course, on a smaller scale) His own boundless power and delight and goodness.

The process will be long and in parts very painful, but that is what we are in for. Nothing less. He meant what He said.[14]

I also read a little book by Sadhu Sundar Singh of India, who was from Punjab.[15] He was from a wealthy family, and he eventually came to know the Lord Jesus Christ. But as a young man without inner peace, he was going to commit suicide. He planned to throw himself in front of a running train that went by his house in the village at about 4:30 in the morning.

The night before, he cried out, "God, if there is a living God, reveal Yourself to me, because I have no reason to live unless I find peace." That night Jesus appeared to him in a vision and told him, "I am the Way, the Truth and the Life." His life was transformed by that encounter, and he became a monk traveling everywhere. His final journey was to preach in Tibet.[16]

But he would live for years alone in the forest, or in a cave like St. Antony, praying and seeking God. And he writes several times about somebody who appeared to him and identified himself as one of the earlier saints. Apparently, Jesus told this individual to go and talk to Sadhu Sundar Singh and to answer the questions he was asking. It sounded a bit like Moses and Elijah appearing before the disciples at the Transfiguration of Christ. Sundar Singh writes that the appointed saint knew all his questions before he asked them. Some questions and answers, the saints told Sundar Singh, he was not allowed to share with anyone or even to keep a physical record of.

In my late 20s when I first encountered his book, I was not able to accept these accounts as real. But now, having read many such stories about the lives of the early Church Fathers, I know what Sundar Singh wrote are not fairy tales or made-up!

An important question we must always be asking ourselves is, "Do I really know God?" For a good part of my ministry, I believe I have been a kind of "good lawyer" for the Lord. I defended Him, explained about Him, and argued for Him. And you know, the strange thing is that in all the writings of the early Church Fathers, there are few materials written to defend God's existence. All that is needed to be said is God *is* the Creator and we are His creation, and we as believers don't ask God to prove Himself to us. We are like little kids. We don't ask our mother and father if they are our parents—we are their children, and they are our parents, and that's it—period! I would say that this is some of what God was leading me to understand from these Church Fathers and their teachings. I certainly don't grasp it all, but it is good to know that God can speak in ways other than just through us reading the Bible or listening to expository sermons. I am not talking about extra revelation contrary to the written Word of God. The Bible is absolute, infallible and all our experience and traditions should *never* contradict the Word of God.

It's fair to say that these men and women of God were also opening up the Scriptures for me in a way beyond what I had known. I was learning from my spiritual forerunners what God had in mind for people like me from the very beginning, from creation itself: that we would be like Him and reflect the Creator.[17]

Here is another truth that, for me, is coming more into focus these days. God is not limited by time and space. The past, present and future are somehow all present to Him. How that can be, I don't know. But for God, these three somehow conjoin.

For example, God could see Peter denying Christ, and, at the same time, He could see Peter as the leader of the apostles and leader of the Church.[18] And He could see the woman who was caught in adultery and brought to Jesus[19] as the godly woman she would be a few months later. You see, God can see the past, the present and the future all as the *now*. So, yesterday's wicked soul could be a saint tomorrow. The same is true today!

My sense is that the early Christians tapped into this way of interpreting life more quickly than those of us who arrived on the scene much later. Any who fight us now, or tend to make our lives miserable, are too quickly classified as the "enemy," and our thinking locks in on that judgment. But I have a feeling that the early Church attempted to view them as potential saints and prayed for them from that perspective.

I know I am still quite earthbound in my thinking. In my mental and physical pain, I had no thoughts where I considered the possibility of those against me ever becoming saints. I didn't even come close to envisioning that in the early days of our forest fire. But I believe a combination of my reading and my suffering has at least brought me to the place where I am now—being willing to die to my good name, and to my reputation of my own righteousness and to embrace the always-loving and forgiving heart of my Maker.

✠ ✠ ✠

Another lesson these men and women of the past were teaching me was about the beauty of the sacramental life—a life lived in union with Christ through physical means. According to historical Christianity, there are seven sacraments, or points of contact, between the visible and the invisible, such as baptism and Holy Communion. A sacrament is a visible sign of an invisible reality. Somehow, although we may not understand exactly how, God meets with us in the physical actions and elements of the sacraments. For example, regarding the Holy Communion (or the Eucharist—from the Greek word meaning "Thanksgiving," often referred to as "The Great Thanksgiving"), Jesus said, "Unless you eat My flesh and drink My blood you have no part in Me."[20]

The sacrifice of Christ that took place 2000 years ago should be understood as the eternal sacrifice. "The lamb that was slain before the foundation of the world."[21] With Almighty God, our past, present, future, time and space, visible and invisible, all are *present* before Him. Hence, when the Church celebrates the Eucharist, it is *not* that we sacrifice Christ again, but the reality, timelessness, continuous effect of the sacrifice is in the present *for* the believing. In that moment, we experience a touch of the divine, and that moment of sacrifice becomes our "now"; past, present and future all the same in the Eucharist.

The Ancient Greeks had two words to describe time. One was *chronos* and the other *kairos*.

While *chronos* is like the flowing river that is continuous—seconds, minutes, hours, weeks, months and years—*kairos* refers to a specific event or experience. Consider the crucifixion of Christ; for Christ, it was His *kairos* experience of time, within the ever continuing *chronos* (*chronology* is derived from *chronos*). *Chronos* is macro time; *kairos* is micro time. Within the history of time (*chronos*), the sacrificial death of Christ took place in the event *in* and *to* history, which was the *kairos* of time.

So, when we participate in the Eucharist, we are experiencing the death of Christ for us as blessed Mary and John the Apostle witnessed at the foot of the Cross. Jesus' death, the pouring out His holy blood, His broken body is *NOW* our *kairos* in the *chronos*. Only God can do it. And Christ is the Godman who gave Himself for our redemption.

One of the most transforming, impacting events in my life was when God in His mercy opened my eyes to *see* the mystery of the Eucharist, that it is more than an image to remember or just an event in history. The Eucharist is *in* the present, and now I am partaking of

His body and blood—the real presence of Christ, the living Word of God is a *kairos* experience for me. Mystery of all mysteries! This understanding transformed my inner life and outer life.

From the beginning of the Church, when God's people gathered for worship, the altar table, Holy Communion, was the center of the gathering; not a pulpit.

Some studies have been released from post-Christian, Western nations indicating that 59 percent of the young people who are raised in contemporary Christian churches end up leaving home when they are 18–19 and *stop* going to church altogether.[22] They completely abandon it. Why is that?

Did they not benefit from the Bible teaching they received week after week? I'm sure in many ways they did. But too often, it simply became head knowledge. It is like someone studying how to go to the moon, and he finally understands every step needed to get there, but never in his life will he attempt to actually go. He knows how to do it, and he keeps that knowledge locked up in his mind. Being taught something is *not* the same as choosing to do that something.

Today our churches are filled with professionals who listen to the many broken families and the grave problems they face, and counsel those families. But in the early Church it was like in the book of James, which reads, "Confess your sins to one another and call the elders of the church."[23] Confession in the Church is like what Nathan did when he dealt with David's sin.[24] The ordained pastor, or priest, hears the confession of the believer who is broken by his transgressions, and the priest says, "Now confess your sins to God." The priest is a witness to listen and give any advice if needed, but also to promise forgiveness on behalf of God, who has already forgiven the one who repented of his or her sin.[25]

When the penitent finishes, the priest asks, "Have you finished honestly confessing your sins to God and decided to make retribution?" When the response is "Yes," then the priest says these wonderful words as he makes the sign of the cross toward the penitent: "In the name of the Father and of the Son and of the Holy Spirit, your sins are forgiven. Go in peace and do not let the enemy hold you in the bondage of guilt anymore. Your past is gone; it shall be remembered no more." As the penitent receives the blessings, they also sign themselves with the sign of the cross. For many, this act of humbling oneself and of outspoken contrition is a powerful moment. The priest is not forgiving the sins himself but reminding the confessor of the Lord's love and forgiveness that has already been given to him. Confession is another of the beautiful, time-honored sacraments of the Holy Church.[26]

Jesus told the disciples, "If you forgive the sins of any, they are forgiven them."[27] For me, this journey of knowing this life of God in my own flesh while I live here on earth is the most exciting thing in the whole world.

✠ ✠ ✠

I have been writing about how God in His providence was always ministering to me, even during these most difficult recent years, through the testimony of the men and women of the early Church. Now once again I am tempted to write the words with which I began this chapter: "…and that's not the half of it." There is so much more I could write, but I have given enough examples for you to at least consider what is being conveyed.

Yes, this crisis of the past few years and all the struggles that are sure to come ahead could go on, but the bottom line is this question: What will it be like when I see Him face to face?

Today I live with one thought in my mind: I am called to build *His* Holy Church. Through this journey of learning from the ancient Church, all of us with the ministry have become more committed than ever to go everywhere possible with the incredible message of Christ. Our focus has become sharper, and my conviction is that our best days of ministry are still ahead of us.

I am aware that if I write a thousand more books or no books at all, if I have millions of dollars in my pocket or not a penny to my name, if I have all the material possessions I could want or not even a roof to sleep under, it means nothing.[28] I really have nothing in the end! All I've truly ever had is skin and bones and a few pounds of flesh, and all I want to know is, *Can this God who dwells in Heaven take this broken heart and allow it to truly experience Him?*[29] The deepest question in my heart is, *Will I continue to hunger to know this God and to grow to be like Him?*

I do not say that my story should be your story. Anyone who knows the Lord can experience this life of theosis—a term used to explain the privilege of participating in the divine nature of God (I will talk more about this in chapter 6). I am only trying to share with you the journey on which He is taking me. It's bloody and difficult, but it's so incredibly beautiful because in the midst of the darkness He shows up, and I see Him and I walk with Him, and I hear Him say, "Follow Me."

☩ ☩ ☩

By understanding the ancient Church and the lives of the people of God, we come to learn that the most sacred entity God has on earth is His Holy Church. Jesus poured out His holy blood for His Church. And God wants us to understand the awesome mystery of the Holy Church so much. As we follow Him, we will sooner or later begin to see this mystery and hunger to be part of it.

The Church can be seen as a chain of links forged over 2,000 years. We, too, are a link in that historical chain that is being forged in our generation. When we see our lives in the light of that chain and the privilege of being part of His living and radiant Holy Church, our personal pain and questions become unimportant. This is what we will learn in the next chapter.

Beautiful, beautiful, beautiful Church!

CHAPTER FIVE

ANOTHER LINK IN THE CHAIN

No one can have God as his father, who does not
have the Church for his mother.

— St. Cyprian of Carthage[1]

A s long as I live, I will never forget the day.

I was young. So were most of our team. We drove a beat-up old van into a village in Southeast Asia, parked it near the market and started giving out tracts. We were friendly and talked to people, inviting them to an open-air meeting later in the day. It was a routine we had followed a few times. We felt we were pretty good at it.

This time was different. It took us a few minutes to realize what was happening. A small but very angry group of religious extremists was attempting to surround us. Once it was obvious that we'd noticed what they were doing, they started shouting at us menacingly.

Then they stepped it up a notch, throwing stones at us. We were outnumbered, trapped, and certainly no match for a group of angry people who obviously had no qualms about using violence, not just words. The best we could hope for was to try to protect ourselves.

They closed in on us, still shouting. We feared for our safety, and our fears were realized when they started hitting us, using their fists with no restraint. Before long, I found myself on the ground, curled up like a ball, which was exactly what they proceeded to kick me like, hard enough to score a winning penalty. We were rescued by people who weren't so violently inclined. They tried to calm things down and pacify the rowdy gang trying to use us for sport. The ruffians dispersed, but not before their leader issued a warning: "Get out of here, and never come back! If you try to, the next time we'll kill you!" He sounded dead serious, so we got up and quickly heeded his warning.

That happened many years ago. Now fast-forward to about five years ago. One of our Episcopas (another name for Bishop, derived from the original Greek)[2] of Believers Eastern Church informed me, "Today we have a consecration* of a new church building, and guess what? It's

---

* To make or declare something or someone (such as a priest or bishop) as holy or sacred—as set apart unto the Lord.

in the very community where many years back you were beaten up for attempting to share the love of Christ!"

Later I was shown pictures of the special occasion where the church building was dedicated, and yes, it was the same community where, decades ago, our young group had been attacked. I felt humbled and deeply grateful to the Lord.

I certainly would not want to repeat that experience of being beaten or anything similar. However, if given the choice, I would prefer the physical persecution over the mental and emotional beatings meted out over the past several years.

Back then in my early journeys with Jesus, never in my wildest dreams would I have imagined that God was going to give birth to a marvelous church movement the way He has through our small beginnings, which has now become international in scope.

That's the story I want to unfold in this chapter.

✟ ✟ ✟

In earlier books, I've written about the positive experience of being a pastor of a local church in the United States. It was after four and a half years among them that I preached my final sermon to these good people. There were tears and hugs that morning as I said goodbye and left to give leadership to a new movement of sorts, to take the love of Christ to people and communities that hadn't yet had the opportunity to hear our Lord's name even one time.

But something strange happened that day as I walked down the steps from the church and to the parking lot. It felt like someone behind me had taken off my jacket. I turned around to see who it was. I realized there was no one there, and of course I was still wearing my jacket. A bit befuddled, I proceeded to walk to my car. After I got in and closed the door, this small voice in my heart said, "Your assignment as the shepherd of my sheep *here* is over. That mantle will be given to another. Now proceed to the new assignment I have for you to do."

I have shared this experience occasionally in my public meetings, and not a single time could I tell this story without choking up, sometimes even crying. Even now as I write this, my throat tightens with emotion. This memory is one of those *kairos* experiences I cannot forget.

Before this moment, I didn't realize the seriousness and the sacredness with which God looks upon His worshiping communities. The years that followed had much to teach me.

✝ ✝ ✝

As a link in the long, unbroken chain (one, holy, catholic and apostolic Church*) that started 2000 years ago, the direct result of missions work that gave birth to the Holy Church, we also began as a mission movement. It was especially focused on sharing the basic message of Christ's love with people who had never before heard the Good News of God's love revealed in the life, death and resurrection of His Son. We believed that in Asia, the answer was to prioritize partnering with the existing Body of Christ already there, rather than sending over workers from the West. This seemed to us the most prudent path, although I've never believed workers from the West are not needed or should be discouraged from going to anywhere they're led as they answer God's call and guidance, especially when there are so many places where so much is work is left to be done. We committed to support, encourage and pray for these brothers and sisters in Asian nations so that they could accomplish the work set before us in the short time we have left.[3] They served in their

---

* This is taken from the Nicene Creed. In this profession of faith, the word *catholic* does not refer to the Roman Catholic denomination, but rather it refers to the timeless Body of Christ that spans nations and denominations.

own culture, going to *near* cultures and *cross*-culturally doing the Great Commission.[4]

This move proved to be breakthrough thinking, and as generous support from around the world was entrusted to our new mission, undeniably incredible results began to be experienced.

Soon we had a new set of problems. How were we to lead the new believers who were now coming to know the Lord in totally unchurched communities? What were we to do? Leave them alone to be independent, like so many others have done, only to see them fall apart without any accountability? Or guide them to be part of the one, holy, catholic and apostolic Church?

There were decisions we needed to make. We worked in preparation of those decisions for two years, steadily and relentlessly, gathering research, learning, understanding, making changes, before it was time to gather together and choose our way forward with finality. Then we held a significant meeting in Nagpur, India, in December 2002. We called on all the 120 senior leaders responsible for our work in South Asia to attend. The gathering was to last for a week, and the purpose was to discuss the future of our ministry.

The chapel that was constructed for this historic gathering is still preserved in the 45-acre Diocesan community in Nagpur.

Paperwork was presented by a team that had been appointed to do extensive research on these matters. Their conclusion was that it was becoming obvious that the best way to move forward was to become a church with episcopal governance. We needed a constitution, Canon Law, a common order of worship (or liturgy), legitimately consecrated bishops and so on. This church is not an independent entity, like a missions organization, but governed by a College of Bishops and responsible, related leaders.[5]

Out of the 120 leaders who attended, only seven disagreed. All others signed their names supporting this new direction. And this was the beginning of Believers Eastern Church as it is known today.

Even as I record this historic event, I can hardly comprehend or believe that, just as in the Book of Acts, the church grew; only God could do it. It is a miracle.

It is amazing to look back and realize that in 2019 GFA World celebrated its 40th year of ministry.

From this small beginning, we now have over 12,000 local congregations established throughout

16 nations representing over 300 languages and, as I already mentioned earlier, a new field will soon be opening in Africa by God's grace. But I am getting ahead of my story.

Quite quickly we were faced with another issue: Who was going to be chosen and consecrated as the first Episcopa and Metropolitan of our church? After talking with some of the leaders of established churches, we knew that whoever was eventually consecrated as such should have theological education and also pastoral experience. These qualifications would not be an issue as there were many individuals who met these requirements.

Another big matter also arose: Which church body with Apostolic Succession* would officially conduct the first Bishop's consecration so that our church might become part of the authentic Church that was begun by the Lord Jesus Christ in AD 33, under the leadership of St. Peter? From Church history we know the Apostolic Succession is a very carefully guarded, unbroken reality, akin to the careful genealogy of Jesus recorded in the Gospels.

---

* The unbroken chain of authority originating from the apostles of Christ.

We believe Jesus appointed (consecrated) the apostles, and St. Peter was given the spiritual authority to lead the Church.[6] The apostles then consecrated and appointed the bishops of the Church, and the Bishops ordained priests to shepherd the local parishes. This Apostolic Succession has maintained the integrity of the doctrines and Holy Traditions of the Church for 2,000 years. Holy Traditions were given to us by the apostles and Church Fathers to show us practical steps to follow in our walk with the Lord.[7]

By church doctrine and tradition, only a head Bishop with two or more other Bishops with him as co-celebrants are authorized to consecrate a new Bishop.

Our next step was to appoint a commission led by one of our most senior leaders, who had secured his Ph.D. from Fuller Seminary in California and whose training had become important to lead this commission. He is now one of the 30 Bishops that lead our church. This commission's job was to research and map out how we could get the consecration done by a responsible church in India. In God's time, the Church of South India (CSI) agreed to consecrate the first bishop of our church for us. CSI is the second-largest church body in India next to the Catholic Church. Its Apostolic Succession comes under the Apostolic See of Rome,* which was one of the five sees of the ancient Church.

The committee picked a senior, godly man for us to have consecrated as our first Bishop and Metropolitan. But when we brought this decision to the Most Rev. Dr. K.J. Samuel, who was then the supreme head of the Church of South India, he simply refused and said to me, "I understand he is qualified. But if we are to do this, we will consecrate you only, and no one else. We know you, your track record, and you are the one who started this movement." I was in trouble, in *deep* trouble. I had never even imagined that I should be the Episcopa or Metropolitan. This idea was so alien to my thinking.

I was heavily influenced by Gandhiji's simplicity and philosophy. Mahatma Gandhiji was the father of India, securing freedom from the 200 years of colonial rule by England. In 1947, when the independence was secured, Gandhiji never wanted to be the president or prime minister of India. *Yes,* I reasoned, *God somehow used me to create a large movement, but that didn't necessarily mean I should be the bishop of the church.*

---

* This name refers to the jurisdiction of the Bishop of Rome. The See of Jerusalem, Antioch, Alexandria, and Constantinople were the other four sees.

It took months for me to realize that, even though I had never wanted nor wished to be the Episcopa or Metropolitan of our church, the 12 most senior leaders of the movement had all decided among themselves that I must be the one consecrated as the first Episcopa and Metropolitan of the church. As time went by, I slowly came to realize this was God's call for me, to lay down my life for the Holy Church. I had to *die* to my reputation and pride. By nature, I was quite private. But finally, one night I knelt by my bed and said, "Lord, I am willing to die to myself, and I surrender all my future plans and willfully choose to do what You seem to be calling me to do for Your Holy Church . . . I will obey the leaders in authority of our movement."

It reminds me of the early morning hours in 1966 in Bangalore, after that evening challenge by George Verwer to surrender my life to serve Him. George's call was to "come, live and die." All that night I could not sleep, deep in pain and fear. Finally, I knelt beside my bed in tears in Clarence High School, where we were staying. "Lord God," I gasped in surrender to His presence and will, "I will give myself to speak for You—but help me to know that You're with me."[8]

✢ ✢ ✢

On February 6, 2003, the consecration took place at our St. Thomas Cathedral in India. I will never forget how my wife Gisela, who is German, with my children, Daniel and Sarah, aged 27 and 23, were there to walk with me from our residence to the Cathedral for the consecration. She was sober and a bit quiet.

But after the consecration was over, she said to me, "*I watched you take the death walk.*"

"Why are you saying that?" I asked.

"I saw you from the time you walked out of the house after praying. You were gloomy. During the whole service you looked like you were a dead man. And when they finally placed the ring on your finger declaring that now you are the shepherd for this church, I saw your face, and I could feel what you were going through. You were doing something that you never wanted to do, but you were also obeying the Lord."

That *is* exactly what happened, and it was like the day I left my local congregation back in Dallas, Texas some years ago. I understood that a heavy, new mantle had fallen on my shoulders to care for His Holy Church, a new link in my generation.

I thank God that long before this event, I personally had already been in a desperate search to know Him and for Him to be more real in my life. Don't misunderstand, I had years of theological training, I had my degrees, and I knew the Bible well. But somehow, there was this concern that I really didn't know *Him* all that well. This longing is what drove me to go back and read the early Church Fathers and study their lives, which I wrote about in the last chapter. So many of them were killed, and yet they had conducted themselves admirably. Hundreds of them would volunteer to be burned to death to protect the Church.

So, I realized there's an Apostolic Tradition, which required me to live out these teachings from the Church Fathers that I had been reading, and I was desperately hungry to learn all that these things meant. But now that I had become the Metropolitan of the church, it was no longer just about my own search to know God. I now felt the weight of the incredible significance of what I had been entrusted with, the responsibility to lead these young believers in the way of the Lord. I found myself spending endless hours in silence. Solitude became part of my spiritual journey, as did fasting and praying in order to learn how I may lead His Holy Church, following in the footsteps of the early Church Fathers.

Although I had my theological education and had served a local parish for a few years, I confess I was not prepared to wear this new "shroud" that was given me. Was it a death garment? I found myself more silent and terribly alone, deep in thought about these many churches and God's people to whom I was now the spiritual father, and the awesome responsibility that was now mine to lead them in the ways of God.

The Church is *one*. There is only *one* head. The Church is called the Body of Christ. The word *body* or *bride* is a singular word. Yet, as we know, this Bride is made up of untold millions from all time *(chronos)*.

The Church Jesus started continued without wavering or compromising the Apostolic doctrines and Holy Traditions, in spite of the hundreds of cults that sprang up, like Arianism, Montanism, Gnosticism, Marcionism and so on.

The purity of the Church was maintained through the Apostolic Succession and Holy Tradition of the Holy Church. When a church starts in any century, if they form a link in the long chain of the authentic Church, then they must follow the Apostolic doctrines and Holy Tradition.[9]

While we don't say others are any less, we just want to say that this is the way that seems right to the "Holy Spirit and to us"[10] for the Believers Eastern Church.

In my private life, I was now even *more* desirous to know God like these saints of old. Reading Dr. Robert Webber's writings helped beyond what words can describe. He wrote about the ancient Church of the first several hundred years,[11] and from him I learned more of what it means to be a leader in His Holy Church.

Studying Church history, we learn that for over 1,000 years from its birth there was only one church. All believed in the apostles' doctrines, the Holy Traditions and the Nicene Creed of AD 325. Unfortunately, the Bishop of Rome felt he must be supreme instead of first among equals (which is the original stand of the early Church). In AD 1054 the Separation of East and West occurred.[12] How sad it was!

The Roman Catholic Church (West) and the Orthodox Church (East) went their separate ways. It wasn't until 1517 that Martin Luther nailed his 95 theses to the church door at Wittenberg, Germany. The Protestant Reformation would end up with numerous denominations, many of them fighting one another. But the Reformation didn't affect the Orthodox Church of the East. They held on to the Apostolic doctrines and Holy Traditions as they still do. Back in England, King Henry VIII had his problems with the Pope in Rome, who would not allow him to leave his wife by annulment. So, in November 1534, King Henry elevated himself to the head of the Church of England in place of the Pope of Rome.[13] How interesting history can be! Believe it or not, Martin Luther's best friend in the Reformation, Zwingli of Zurich, and he became bitter enemies over their disagreement over the meaning of the Eucharist. While Luther believed the Eucharist is a mystery with Christ's real presence, Zwingli opposed it as just a reminder. They separated ways.

> Indeed, Luther went so far as to liken the presence of the sun in creation to the presence of the Son in Communion: "At Creation God ordained that the sun must daily rise and shine and give light and warmth to creatures. Just so the Lord Christ also ordained and commanded that in His church His essential body and blood are to be present in the Lord's Supper, not merely in a spiritual but also in a bodily and yet incomprehensible manner."[14]

✛ ✛ ✛

A few years after our church began, I felt the need to write *The Guiding Principles* about our core beliefs.[15] It is for new believers to understand matters such as how when we come together for worship, we need to realize that worship is already going on, and we are now joining with the angels and archangels and saints of Heaven, and God *is* the audience. The Holy Trinity is the center of everything, not the pulpit, or the instruments. We are primarily focused on worshiping God.

But there is a question that needs to be addressed: In our commitment to remain pure and Orthodox, holding to what the Church has believed from the beginning, did we dilute our passion to serve people in parts of the globe where His name was often never heard? The truth of the matter is our hearts were, and are, even more burdened and passionate to bring the love of Christ to such peoples. We as a church recognize that one of our *traditions* is going to be studying Acts, not just as a theological book, but as a blueprint. It is an account of *how* the church must function when modeling the love of Christ, healing the sick, casting out demons and sharing the Good News about men and women being reconciled with God. So, our vision only got bigger and more committed. Since Jesus died for the whole world, we have no excuse and hold nothing back to take this message to the whole world.

For me, I am grateful for this season of life where I function as the Metropolitan of the church. My greatest longing is still for the 2 billion people in our generation who wait to hear that Jesus died for them to have the freedom to make an informed choice to love Him, to follow Him and to become part of His Holy Church.

Any mission that seeks to follow the ways of the apostles will learn from what happened in Acts 2. St. Peter explained the love of Christ, and 3,000 people committed their lives to Him and the Church was born.[16] Then in Acts 13 you find that, as the Church in Antioch was in worship, the Holy Spirit had them send out apostles Paul and Barnabas to go to the ends of the world to bring the Good News.[17] That's how missions works, and it is like what happened to GFA. We went out to do the Great Commission as was done by the apostles, and hundreds of local churches were born as a result of it.

A true biblical mission never remains a mission. It will always transform itself into a church, and those churches will then send out more missionaries. I am amazed as I look back on all that's happened. This progression is absolutely biblical, but it's nothing I ever planned to happen. We simply said, "God, You do what You want to do with us. We are like the dry leaves in the wind that You blow along." What we have seen during these years is nothing short of an absolute miracle. Hearing the stories taking place on the mission field right now really is like living in the days of the Book of Acts.

✠ ✠ ✠

A story is told of three stone cutters who were at their job in Italy. A foreign tourist, seeing their hard work, asked the first stone cutter what he was doing? He replied, "Can't you see what I am doing? This is my profession. I am very good at what I do, cutting this massive stone into beautiful shape, I am skilled to know how to do it. These are the tools I use." He boasted of his years of craftsmanship and ability.

The tourist asked the second man, who was in the same vicinity, what he was doing. He answered, "This is my job, to make a living. I do my job with great care, and I get paid very well for what I do."

The third man was asked the same question, "What are you doing?" Looking up into the eyes of the enquirer, the stone cutter replied, "I am building a cathedral for my God."

Think about it. All of them were skilled, well-trained, doing the same job, but the "why"—their reasons, their purposes—were different. For the first one, it was his craft; the second one, his payment and reward. But for the third one, his reason was something beyond his profession, craft and payment; he saw that one day the stone he had beautifully cut into the right size would help to build the cathedral for His God, and many would gather to worship God in His Holy Church![18]

In this world of missions, there is a deception that has taken place. For the past several hundred years, thousands of mission organizations with sincere hearts set out to fulfill the Great Commission,[19] but the particular jobs they performed—radio broadcasts, translation work, social work, literature ministry, starting up seminaries, etc.—became seen as an end in themselves rather than being recognized as simply the means to establish local churches. Most mission organizations remained non-denominational so their fundraising from multiple denominations would be unaffected.

We must realize, the "tools" have a limited shelf life. It doesn't take much research to see how hundreds of mission organizations that once thrived are now not operational.

St. Paul, St. Barnabas and the others started the missionary work with the end in mind—that is to establish local churches directed by the Antiochian See of the Church.

Those churches that kept their apostolic communion and lineage sent out missionaries to do missions and plant churches, like the church in Antioch.

All forms of outreach are good and needed, but if they are not done with the deep understanding of why we do them—to establish a local church according to Apostolic doctrines and Holy Traditions—then we miss the heart of the Great Commission.

Unfortunately, at least in the past, a few mission movements were set up according to what might be called a *business model:* They go and "give out" the Gospel and then leave. The letters of the New Testament tell us a different story of how those men and women did what they did to become part of the community and establish a church.

Please don't misunderstand me, I am not saying all failed. Many understood this principle and established local churches all over the world. The Orthodox Church, Catholic Church and Anglican Church are a few examples of those who did understand, along with many others.

Years ago, we began as a mission that evolved into a church, according to the Apostolic doctrines and Holy Traditions. The journey continues, going where no one has gone before, doing what Jesus told His apostles to do until He returns.[20]

During Roman times, many were executed by means of crucifixion. Jesus was also among them. What makes the Cross of Christ different, then?

It is *who* Christ was. The Almighty God in flesh, the sinless Son of God being crucified as the sacrifice to redeem mankind by pouring out His own Holy Blood.[21] The death of Christ was *not* the end in itself; it was for a purpose, that is to establish His Church, His Bride.

So, all that we do must have a focus and deep understanding—whatever we do should end in seeing a local, worshiping church established.

✠ ✠ ✠

I began this chapter with a short story. Allow me to end that way as well. Our local diocese sent out two seminary graduates as evangelists to a certain area for ministry. One was Joseph, and his coworker was named John. Soon the anti-Christian group started to cause problems, and eventually a group of them came and surrounded both Joseph and John. One took out a long dagger and stabbed Joseph. He fell, blood pooling around him. He could not be revived and soon died. They also stabbed John, but he lived. He was taken to the hospital, and it took months for him to recover.

Recently, when I visited the particular mission field where this tragedy happened, it was deeply moving to witness the local church that got established in the very community where evangelist Joseph had lain in a pool of his own blood. Tertullian, one of the early Church fathers, famously said, "the blood of the martyrs is the seed of the Church."[22] Yes, the new Christians now have a church building on the place where he was martyred. A strong congregation is functioning as a living testimony to the love of God. It was also a joy for me to meet John, who continues to serve his Lord, and is willing to pay any price to get the job done.

As the Word of God says, Jesus poured out His Holy Blood for the sake of His Church.[23]

How little we really understand of the magnitude of this great mystery.

✞ ✞ ✞

After reading what I write here about *my own* journey to the ancient Church, one might easily misunderstand and think that I don't value the protestant denominations. The truth is that, while I am grateful for my journey, I believe God's precious people are there in all denominations. Martin Luther, Zwingli, John Stott and Billy Graham are only a few examples of godly people who have followed Him. And there is no reason for discrimination or fighting among the people of God. The highest peak of theology *is* God. All theology is about Him. There is nothing beyond that. And the Word says, "God *is* love."[24] Even if the way we think differs, if our hearts are full of love for the Lord and for people we will not end up like the Pharisees, who strongly believed they had all the right doctrines and carefully followed the traditions handed down to them from their fathers *yet* were alienated from God! If it were not for the hundreds of protestant denominations that helped us to reach the world with Christ's love, GFA World would *not* exist today. Let not our personal convictions destroy the unity and love we have in Christ.

✛ ✛ ✛

Deception and pitfalls are many in this journey to meet Christ one day. False prophets and cults abound. Knowing the truth about the authentic Holy Church is not enough; we must *become* part of it. The ultimate goal of God for His people is for us to become like His Son, the Lord Jesus Christ. Embracing sacramental life is how the grace of God will change us from within. Our church gatherings for worship have one true purpose: to behold the One who is among His people and worship Him and be transformed by the power of the Holy Spirit. That is what we learn in our journey into the next chapter. It is not too late for us to return to the old ways.

Return to the old ways.[25]

CHAPTER SIX

HUNGER FOR REALITY

We should have no other object but God in our actions and seek to please Him alone in all things.
— St. Vincent de Paul[1]

Recently, I was in England where I love to see the old churches. During my travels to cities like York, Oxford and, of course, London, I'm always fascinated by these 1,200-year-old structures. I walk in and quietly imagine the presence of the many people throughout the generations who worshiped there.

The architecture and the atmosphere remind me of Isaiah 6 when worship is depicted, and you see the entire focus on the One who sits on the throne:

> I saw the Lord, sitting on a throne, high and lifted up, and the train of his robe filled the temple. Above it stood seraphim; each one had six wings: with two

he covered his face, with two he covered his feet, and with two he flew. And one cried to another and said: "Holy, holy, holy is the LORD of hosts; the whole earth is full of his glory!" (Isaiah 6:1–3).

In those old stone churches, I can see these Christians down throughout the centuries gathering together, with one voice singing praises, saying the Creed in unison, partaking in Holy Communion, and then being sent out as His witnesses in the world.

During a recent trip, I had an unforgettable experience. I was standing just outside an old church, lost in the beauty of the design and the construction, when the guide pointed out that it was no longer a church. It was now a *pub!* I was in shock.

☩ ☩ ☩

I grew up by the riverbanks in a tiny village in the very southern part of India. I remember as a little boy the coconut trees that grew nearby and leaned over the wide river. We kids would climb up those trees and then jump into the water and swim. But here's the thing—from the height of those coconut trees we could look down where the water was clear and see the river bottom.

Today, however, if you went with me to see that same river, you'd find it dirty and polluted. What happened? Well, over the past 50 years, hundreds of homes were built along the river, and with more people, more pollutants were dumped into the river so that there is now no life left in the river. It is dead.

In some ways, I see this as an analogy for what's been happening in so many places to physical church buildings, yes, but also to the non-physical Church. Think about it. Two thousand years ago, the Church was born—it was orthodox, true and faithful to the Word and to the instructions of the Lord Jesus and the way He lived in the world. But as time went on, people began to dump their various opinions, methods and teachings into the Church, and now so much of what we see today is no longer the thing of beauty He intended.

But now go back with me to my river. We'll get in a canoe and paddle to the headwaters. As we travel near where the stream starts, we will find water that is still clear and clean and pure. Going back to the start is what I believe we need to do regarding the Church. We can't simply go back 500 years to the Reformation and think we're at the beginning. We need to return to the real beginning, the early centuries.

✝ ✝ ✝

It is reported in the media that thousands of churches are being closed in England and, unfortunately, most of them are bought by non-Christians to set up bars and create other businesses.[2] They could become a dance hall or a museum, a liquor store or a restaurant.

It troubles me that the great, rich church heritage in these countries, which is so beautiful, could be treated with what seems to be such little respect.

I've thought to myself somewhat facetiously, *If turnabout is fair play, maybe a group of committed English believers should get together and buy a famous restaurant . . . and then turn it into a church!*

In all seriousness, the information I read and the church buildings I saw used for other purposes troubled me deeply. But I had to make a deliberate effort not to think about it. I had to stay focused on bringing His name to the people of our generation who are waiting to find out that there is a God who loves them.

This more restricted point of concentration was also beginning to reflect what I felt about other places around the world. There had been a growing sense in my heart and mind these past years that contemporary Christianity is going to face a massive crisis in the not-so-distant future. It won't be with swords and loaded guns. It will be much more severe.

The Holy Scripture says there will be "a great falling away"[3] where those who believed they were true

Christians are faced with a test, and suddenly, they find they can no longer stand, and they fall apart. I think about some of the trials those like our brothers and sisters in China face today, many of whom I have met during my travels. If they are caught having a meeting in a place that is not government-authorized, they will be punished. Or remember the story in Libya that made such big news? Twenty Coptic Orthodox Christians who refused to deny Christ were marched to the beach and beheaded.[4]

What did these believers have that we are missing? We no longer know what is true and authentic and what is not.

A few years ago, I spent a whole year traveling throughout North America and Europe, speaking almost every Sunday. You wouldn't believe the endless miles I traveled. But at the end of it, I was somewhat sad. You might ask why.

The overall lack of the fear of God saddened me! In some churches where the Eucharist (Holy Communion) was served, how quickly it was done and how casually it seemed to be received. And in a few places, it was not even included as part of the worship service. I felt the music or the preaching had become the main center of attraction rather than the wounded Lamb[5] who sits on the throne. The reverence with which worship should be approached had turned into something more akin to exuberance. In some places, it was difficult to differentiate between what was meant to be a group of God's holy people gathering together and some secular social gathering, music concert or TED-Talk-type of gathering. A charismatic man was the center and the reason why masses were gathering, surely *not* God.

It's possible my reaction could have been due to being tired out from all the traveling. I also know I must fight being overly critical. Others have warned me before against it, and I know I must be vigilant. Even so, I felt a bit like Jeremiah of old. His message was: "Thus says the LORD: 'Stand in the ways and see, and ask for the old paths, where the good way is, and walk in it; then you will find rest for your souls' " (Jeremiah 6:16).

He said this in so many ways and to anyone in Jerusalem who would listen to him. You can't snub your nose at God and not expect to pay a terrible price. The people of Jerusalem who Jeremiah was talking to needed to learn from the past.

I get that Jeremiah's one-point sermon got on people's nerves. He only had that single theme. Maybe people thought he needed to branch out. But God told His prophet that there would be no second sermon until the people in Jerusalem responded to the first one.

This is a severe statement, but maybe the crisis of today is that our modern Christianity has failed to understand the reality of the Christ of the New Testament, and instead has created an entirely *new* Christ and a whole different church.[6]

✠ ✠ ✠

Before I understood the early Church fathers and their teachings, there was a time in my life I was frustrated and angry with the whole world that didn't think like I did. But then, as I began to learn about the privilege God had given me from 2 Peter 1:4 to "partake of His divine nature," my thinking began to change.

Have you noticed? There are brilliant defenders of the faith and even those conducting debates to prove the existence of God. When we listen to them, we go away absolutely thrilled and excited to hear the dozens of arguments to prove their points, just like a brilliant lawyer would argue for his client.

However, when it comes to the invisible, Almighty God who lives outside of time, space and matter, the most important question of all questions is whether we humans, who are created by God to reflect His image, have a direct and living encounter with Him on a concrete and personal level.

Adam and Eve were created without sin. They knew God, but that knowledge and relationship was still in an infant stage. If they had not disobeyed God, they would have grown as a child grows, from an infant to an adult, in an expanding knowledge and experience of their Creator. We don't know exactly what that would have looked like, but being made in the image of God and created by God, the privilege was for them to share in Him and all His divine energy and grow from glory to glory, reflecting His glory through their earthen vessels.[7]

This transformation is exactly what we need as a new creation in Christ.

For quite a few years now, I have been on this beautiful journey of knowing the Lord with the understanding of theosis.

Let me try to explain this briefly.

The aim of the Father is that we may become like His Son.[8] St. Paul talks about how the Holy Spirit changes us from within to become like the Word (Christ) we see in the Scripture.[9]

The early Church Fathers explained this reality using the terms *theosis* and *deification*. According to them, the final goal and the objective for a believer is to become "god," to attain "deification," by sharing in His divine nature. The early Church Father Athanasius is the one who first states that "God became human that we might be made god."[10]

Now, *deification* or theosis never means that man *becomes* God, the Creator. The idea must be understood in light of the difference between the Creator and creation—they can never be the same. The ancient Church, led by the early Orthodox Fathers, rejected all forms of pantheism. As Bishop Kallistos Ware, an Orthodox theologian, explains, this partaking of His divine nature that Peter talks about is union with God's *energies*, not His *essence*. He says, "The mystical union between God and humans is a true union, yet in this union Creator and creature do not become fused into a single being."[11]

When we experience theosis, he goes on to say, we remain distinct (though not separate) from God, and we never stop being human. By God's grace and mercy—through the power of the Holy Spirit—we live in this world as Christ lived. The difference is Christ was without a sinful nature and never sinned, for He was God, the Creator. But also, being fully man, just as we are, He chose to live on earth in accordance with the Father's will.

Our body, soul and spirit continually change,[12] and we are transformed to live as Christ as we yield our lives continually as living sacrifices[13] and embrace the sacramental life, which again is a life lived in union with Christ.[14]

Let me share with you a memory from my childhood about a blacksmith I used to visit. When I was a small boy, studying in the fourth or fifth grade, we kids used to go to the blacksmith in our village and watch him work. We were terribly excited about the sparks that would fly when he struck hot iron with his hammer. We would watch him put this cold metal into the blazing fire. After a few minutes, it would disappear! In actuality, the color of this iron and the fire had become one. We used to think he had lost it in the fire, but before we knew it, he would pull it out, strike it into shape, and then dip into the water with a "hisssssss." Then he would pull it out and repeat the whole process again, over and over.

Becoming like Jesus in our lives is as it was in the life of Jesus. God and man—two separate wills, two separate natures, but in one person—He had both a human will and divine will. Jesus became fully man without ever ceasing to be fully God. The Almighty God was now in human flesh.[15]

It is just like the hot iron. It did *not* ever become the hot flame, *nor* did the fire become the iron. What happened was the iron, being in the flame, took on the nature of the fire. The heat and energy of the fire was imparted *to* the once cold and shapeless iron. This analogy helps us to understand the two natures of Jesus: Jesus laid down His own God powers to obey, as a perfect man, only His Father's will through absolute submission and obedience.[16] This is the reason He could say to His disciples, "He who has seen Me, has seen the Father."[17] He always reflected the Father's image. We are going back to the beginning—"in the image of God."[18]

Through this understanding of theosis, we understand that God is not a God of perfect people who only do right and never sin. No. He is the God of Jacob. It's funny, isn't it? When God talks about Himself, He says He is "the God of Abraham, the God of Isaac, and the God of Jacob."[19] What an encouraging thought! In all of us there is some of Abraham, who lies and tries to save himself, and some of Isaac, who is self-centered and self-focused, and some of Jacob, who is a liar and deceiver and wasted 20 years of his life unbroken and self-centered. But God doesn't say that He is the God of Israel, the transformed saint, but rather He *is* the God of Jacob, the struggling failure.

If that is the case, if God is so merciful to those who are struggling, I must ask the question: Are we looking at the real Church when Christians and church media and Christian bloggers and religious magazines turn against each other and stab each other in the back continually? I have great concerns about the contemporary church we see today, not just in the West, but worldwide. There is a massive deception of Lucifer taking place among us, which seeks to divide and devour from within.

Remember, the enemy is the "accuser of our brethren."[20] This is the spirit of the age we are witnessing. Of course, none of us is without sin. One of the most important books released in recent times is *Messiology* by George Verwer. (It also goes by the name *More Drops* in some places, which is the version published by our church in India.)[21] The book's central message focuses on how God mysteriously works in the midst of the mess and chaos of our lives and the lives of those around us. I highly recommend you get a copy and read it. Look at how much the first century Church, those seven churches that St. John writes to in Revelation, struggled! But Jesus gave them hope. So why is it that today we are so quick to turn on one another? Christian magazines attack each other and the church left and right. Christian organizations sue each other and destroy one another. One of the most significant, godly organizations with a huge impact on the youth in North America was shut down because another Christian organization filed a case against them. How sad! Churches criticize and blame and attack other churches that don't agree with them. I could give you example after example of pastors and churches and organizations that have been destroyed by their so-called fellow Christians.

This phenomenon is exactly what happened to us these past few years. But as I've looked around, I've realized we are far from unique. There is a true conspiracy of Lucifer to destroy the Church from the inside out.

✝ ✝ ✝

When we listen to the heart of Jesus, in His prayer just before going to the cross, He says, "Father, I pray they will be one as We are one."[22] His desire was for us to be as unified together as He and the Father are in the Holy Trinity. And if we look back, we see He gave us the blueprint for us to live as He desires. How are we to win the world? He said, "Love one another as I have loved you, then they will know you belong to me."[23] Although He is stating it differently, Jesus is saying exactly what the apostles taught about life transformation: It starts from the inside out. Light attracts moths. Even if you don't say a word, when you emanate the otherworld life of the living God, which is full of love, peace, forgiveness, passion, concern, care and a deep understanding of grace and mercy, people are drawn to you. If that life of the living God became the life of our churches today, can you imagine what we would see happen?

Once we understand that Jesus called us to love others in this way, we will no longer look at other brothers, sisters and churches as enemies, regardless of the differences we have.

It is important to keep in mind that the goal of God for His Church, which Jesus gave His precious body and blood for, is transformation. We read in Romans 8:29 that the aim is for all those who believe in Christ to become like Jesus.

I am convinced by the teachings of St. Paul that what had happened to the people in Corinth was that they had begun to drift away because following Christ was not easy. The way of the Cross is difficult.[24] So, they chose to interpret Christ as a softer version, and Apostle Paul said, "You are following another Jesus."[25]

I, for one, pray that the contemporary Christian world will wake up to the reality that we are a more lost and broken people than some of the people we are trying to evangelize. I know this sounds controversial and even like one of those conspiracy theories, but let me ask one question: How many more thousands of sermons must be preached and heard before we realize that nothing is getting better; things are only getting worse?

We need to realize that what we are trying to do is to change ourselves and others by our own efforts. This effort is described in Philippians 3 where St. Paul says, "I, by human reason, am the most righteous human being by every standard,"[26] and then, "finally I entered into the mystery of God and found out I don't want to seek my own righteousness."[27] It's the process of God changing us from within and transforming us so that we reflect the love, mercy and kindness of God, rather than being someone who uses any form of manipulation to try and bring about change. God doesn't work that way. We are nothing but lifeless clay, and only the potter can give shape and meaning to us.[28] No matter how hard the clay might fight or struggle, it can accomplish nothing with its own fight or strife.

✢ ✢ ✢

There was a time when I was convinced by the disciple-ship movement. I wrote books and preached sermons about it. But now I look back and realize some of those things I taught were true and powerful, *but* there was something significant missing from all of it. You might be thinking, "Why would you say that? What happened to you?"

The worst deception of Lucifer and his demons is that you can take the Bible and look at all the lists of dos and don'ts and then strive to do those things in your own strength and come across looking like a holy person who never does anything wrong. The problem is that the source is *not* God, but self.[29]

With the human soul's power and energy and a good mind, you can build something that looks to be totally right and perfect in the eyes of the onlooker. But in the end, it's filled with bitterness, anger, jealousy, self-centeredness and a lack of willingness to suffer and sacrifice. A church can appear to be a church with mega success, and yet God may have nothing to do with it. Watchman Nee talks about this brilliantly in his book *The Release of the Spirit.*[30]

There is one blueprint for authentic discipleship and that is the book of Acts, which is a 30-year-long, historical document that tells us about the faith and practices of the early Christians. To remain part of the true Church today in any culture, we must seek to follow the pattern we read in the book of Acts. There you read the reality of the power of the Holy Spirit-filled life through the Church—enduring persecution, suffering for the sake of Christ, embracing a life of prayer, performing miracles and wonders, engaging in sacrificial giving, continually caring for one another, loving people more than their own lives, completely focused on missions with a driving passion for the hurt and dying millions, worshiping with all sincerity, and hundreds of other attributes that you will find outlined as you study the Acts of the Apostles.

✛ ✛ ✛

Recently, I heard a well-known American preacher say to a large gathering of people, in a civic-auditorium setting, that the United States is in the greatest revival their country has ever known.

Wow, I said to myself, *I must have missed something.*

I thought I was in the loop on matters like this. It could be that I am spending too much time in Asia. I know we have been seeing signs of authentic revival in many parts of my own country. But I wasn't aware that *revival* had broken out across North America as well!

Genuine revival is always marked by an overwhelming sense of the presence of the Lord. In a given church, it's almost like Jesus Himself is once again physically present.

Say on a given Sunday morning the risen Christ were to suddenly appear. I believe people would quickly be on their knees before Him. Kneeling is the body language of worship. Some would probably be prostrate in the aisles. Quiet would settle over the sanctuary. Maybe someone would start to sing a song in adoration and others would join in.

I think about the many new worship songs that have marked the modern Church in recent years. Is this the sign of something special starting to take place, another awakening of some kind?

But what about great sorrow over sin?

A wonderful new demonstration of love between Christians?

All kinds of repentance and new believers turning to the Lord—revivals are always marked by countless new Christians.

And people gathering for prayer; you never have revival without prayer being restored to its proper place in the church. Is that being seen?

Is concern for the poor and the powerless starting to manifest itself in these churches?

No, I can't agree—it's not the time of another revival in the West—not yet, anyway.

If only it were, though. But at present, such a comment, even from a respected preacher, is *not* consistent with what we know of past times of authentic awakening.

✛ ✛ ✛

When I am asked about the future of the Church, my mind automatically thinks about the church in these Asian countries like Nepal, Myanmar and Sri Lanka. My great hope is to see a marvelous, Heaven-sent revival in these places, as well as in the West. I believe with all my heart that not only can this kind of revival take place, but in some places in "my world" it is already happening.

When I think of the church in the West, what comes to mind is the incredible generosity of God's people there. It is truly remarkable. Over and over, past and present, GFA has been the fortunate recipient of the Lord working through these faithful believers who have stood behind our brothers and sisters in Asia in so many ways. Like the Apostle Paul writes in Philippians 1:3 (NLT), "Every time I think of you, I give thanks to my God."

But what has gone unnoticed is the *massive* satanic plot I have been describing, which has been unleashed to destroy the Church at large.

Think about it.

Peter denied Christ just like Judas did. Jesus spoke to him harshly, but later Jesus found Peter when he had given up his ministry and gone back to his old boats and nets. Jesus found him and sat with him, asking, "Do you love me?" Jesus never said one thing about how Peter had denied Him or tried to make him feel like an idiot or judged him or condemned him—none of those things. He simply asked if he loved Him.[31] I've painfully come to realize how much of our Christianity today comes together one moment with great singing and clapping of hands and then all too quickly, the very next moment, turns out to be nothing more than wolves in sheep's clothing. When problems come (and they will come), these people who were singing just five minutes ago turn on one another with biting and merciless attacks. Surely this cannot be the mark of the true Christian Church for which Jesus gave His life.[32]

✝ ✝ ✝

Before closing this chapter, I would like to come back and just talk to you, dear reader. You know, when you read the four Gospels and find out the terms Jesus used to describe those who are His, you see things like "denying self" and "picking up your cross daily." Unless we do these things, He said, we cannot be His disciples.[33]

This life of true Christianity is not as simple as saying a few words and believing that's all there is to it, and you're now guaranteed to be Heaven-bound. That's a very dangerous way of thinking. It is good that you become responsible for learning about the ways of Christ and learn from the Orthodox Fathers of the Church and the lives of the followers of Christ in the Book of Acts, because in the end, you and I are not of this world. There's so much more to this journey with the Lord than simply saying a prayer or having some spiritual experience. There is a continual yielding that must take place as we abide in Christ and let His life flow through us.

Jesus came not only to deliver us from sin but to deliver us from our own self-centeredness. I would end here by saying that one of the things that helped me was taking the time to read and study St. Paul's epistles and to study the early Church. It's time to go back to the beginning and to remember the end result is to be made into His image.

Hear the words of Christ: "As the Father has sent me, so I am sending you" (St. John 20:21, NLT).

✝ ✝ ✝

It is unfortunate that Satan, the master deceiver, has blinded the eyes of so many followers of modern Christianity from seeing the glorious face of the One who sits on the throne and is the only reason for our gathering—God. He is the audience for our worship. But man has replaced Him, and now "God is in the dock"[34] as C.S. Lewis put it. St. Paul talked about the ravaging wolves[35] or in other words fake churches in the wings, waiting to destroy God's people. On this journey, we will run into a lot of look-alikes, but we must remember they are only imitations.

Surely the way of discernment is to fix our eyes on the Lord Jesus[36] and to stay true to being part of the Holy Church. In the next chapter I write more about this.

God is the audience in true worship.

✌

CHAPTER SEVEN

LOOK-ALIKES

In many churches Christianity has been watered down until the solution is so weak that if it were poison it would not hurt anyone, and if it were medicine it would not cure anyone!

— A.W. Tozer [1]

Several years ago, one of our Believers Eastern Church Dioceses in South Asia purchased a 100-bed hospital from a businessman, with the goal of serving the poor and needy and demonstrating to them the love of Christ. This hospital was already in operation when we bought it, so our people wanted to make sure everything was functioning well, and that the medicines given out from the hospital pharmacy were all authentic and real. Our medical doctors and management team got professional help to examine and verify all steps and processes across departments. To their surprise, they learned that 50 percent of the medicines were not authentic. They were placebos.

When I found out, I said, "I can't believe it!" One of the first things our staff did after they took over the hospital was to destroy all the fakes. Of course, they also changed the whole system, and today everything functions with a godly worldview, "Whatever you want men to do to you, do also to them."[2] In other words, if you don't want others to hurt you or cause damage to you, then you won't bring harm to them. Love them as you love yourself.[3]

The world is filled with look-alikes. Jesus warned us that there would even be false prophets or preachers. He said they would fool a lot of people. Without discernment, false prophets can appear to be the real thing. Even more serious than that, Scripture tells us that Satan himself has made his followers to look like real servants of God.[4]

During the time of Jeremiah (a true prophet of God), the land of Judah was full of fake prophets, all preaching the exact opposite of what Jeremiah was saying. Jeremiah's messages were *not* popular. He was beaten up by bullies for the words he preached. He was eventually put in stocks and then imprisoned by the king. But he was the only one speaking the truth.

Today, in some places, we have people behind church pulpits who may be speaking clever and impressive words, but they don't always know the Living God. They can sound like the real thing, but unfortunately, they are deceptive and false, just like the hospital medicine I told you about. It looked authentic, but it wasn't. People who suffered were not being healed.

St. Paul wrote this warning to the church in Corinth: "But I am afraid that, as the serpent deceived Eve by his craftiness, your minds will be led astray from the simplicity and purity of devotion to Christ" (2 Corinthians 11:3, NASB).

Anything that dilutes our love for Christ or takes our focus off Him and His ways should concern us. That's enemy talk. So, what is the answer? You must keep your attention on Jesus and the Holy Trinity alone, which is why being part of an authentic church is such an important protection if we are to reach our goals in this journey of faith.[5]

All that glitters is not gold. You cannot look at a horse and call it a man. Human beings don't look like horses. People have two legs, not four. They speak words. They don't go *neigh!*

Just because a lot of people gather in a building, sing songs, pray and use the Bible as a good book from which to teach, does *not* always mean it is an authentic church. The charismatic speaker may even talk about Jesus, but that does *not* mean he is representing the real Christ in the Holy Trinity. The Apostle Paul stated that congregations like this were not as discerning as they should be. They were deceived by charismatic, brilliant and convincing preachers, drawing followers for their own personal gain.[6]

False (or diluted) doctrine is the reason we should make sure the community we are part of acknowledges and follows the Apostolic teachings, Holy Traditions and worship patterns handed down to us from the beginning. Why is Believers Eastern Church proclaimed as orthodox in our faith and worship? Because we strive to adhere to the ancient Church that was begun in the first century.

The Apostolic teachings and Holy Traditions gave birth to what is called the Nicene Creed. That was back in AD 325. It is our plumb line of faith.* It is recited during the Divine Liturgy in worship every Sunday during our Believers Eastern Church worship service.

---

* A *plumb line* is a tool that consists of a small, heavy object attached to a string or rope and that is used to see if something (such as a wall) is perfectly vertical. It is a measuring tool to make sure we're on the right path.

For a church that wants to stay true, it is important to embrace the ancient Nicene Creed, which is the summary of the whole Bible on a single page.[7]

Did you know the Nicene Creed and the teachings of the apostles were the baselines the early Church used when they chose which books would later become the New Testament, or the second part of the Bible? Only years later was the New Testament accepted and canonized as Scripture. It was St. Athanasius, the Bishop of Alexandria, who was the first to formally codify the 27 New Testament books that were canonized as God's Word in AD 367.[8]

The true Church is *not* just individuals worshiping God on their own. True worship begins with God's people responding to His call to gather where the Lord Himself is the audience—together, with their attention fixed on the Holy One who sits on the throne. *God* is the object of true worship. For us in Believers Eastern Church, and for many other churches that hold to orthodox faith and practices, this means both the priest and the congregation physically face the altar (where the Holy Communion is held) during much of the service. This is a tangible way to help direct our visual attention from ourselves and onto the Lord. Also, it speaks visually—the priest or pastor is *not* the mediator between God and His people. The priest *is part of* the worshiping community, with a special call to lead the sheep following the Great Shepherd.

✝ ✝ ✝

Do you remember reading about theosis in the last chapter? Our reason for being alive here on the earth is to be transformed into the image of Christ—to become more and more like Him. As I began to describe earlier, by partaking in His divine nature, our very life is changed by God as we grow into His likeness.[9]

The transformation that takes place through this life of theosis not only changes us on the inside but causes us to see the world through God's eyes. The church at Antioch experienced transformation in their lives and then immediately saw the need to send two people on a missionary journey.[10] In Isaiah 6, Isaiah was in God's very presence when he received his instruction to be sent out.[11]

It is only when we come before Him with open hearts, ready to obey, that we learn what we must do, how we should see differently, and our hearts are able to be transformed by the Holy Spirit—a transformation that is always for the sake of the world into which He sent His beloved Son.

As I said earlier, the Holy Trinity should be the center of our attention. But if we miss seeing Him, if we never really worship *HIM,* then what are we doing? What is the point of our gathering? My concern is that we, as the Church of God, might be deceived and, in the end, find that we missed the whole point, because we never truly met with the Living God!

✠ ✠ ✠

In the book of Nehemiah, we read about people who were confused and lost. But hearing God's Word was what enlightened their hearts, and repentance came as they returned to the Lord.[12] In the ancient Church, they always had at least four readings from God's Word. This included a passage from the Old Testament, one from the Psalms, another from the Epistles, and finally one from the Gospels. That way, throughout the life of the believers (many of whom were illiterate), they would hear the entire Word of God read to them over and over.[13]

The Bible is God's primary way of speaking to us—that we may learn to fear Him and obey Him as the Holy Spirit convicts our hearts. At the same time, we must keep in mind that the Scripture is not meant for individual interpretation, or for each of us to just read it and do what is right in our own eyes. The early

Church believed that it is the Church that interprets the Scripture. The New Testament came out of the Church, not the other way around. When individuals began to interpret the Scripture based on their own reasoning, we find the cause of the over 42,000 denominations that can be found in the Christian world today, each one claiming to be the one true Church. Almost all cults started as Bible study gatherings where one or more individuals interpreted the Word instead of seeking knowledge from what the Church represents through what the Church Fathers and what the seven early Church councils said about it.[14]

✝ ✝ ✝

If you look up the definition of the word "source," you will find other words like, "the spring," "beginning," "fount," "cause," etc.[15]

In Leviticus 10, we find an account in which God's response seems illogical and unreasonable. He had instructed the people of Israel in the way of using incense as part of worship of Him. Incense represents the prayers of God's people. But in this account, a problem occurred when the sons of Aaron (who were some of those authorized to do the censing) needed to find some fire to start the censor. It could be that they had to go a little far to get the fire from the altar where the sacrifices were made, and maybe they thought it was bothersome. So instead, in the words of today, they just took a match and lit it. Whatever way they did it, they essentially were saying, "Fire is fire, it doesn't matter where it's from as long as we achieve the end goal," but God was looking for the censing to take place the way He wished it, and that His will be accomplished.

What happened next? God struck them dead instantly. It says that it was because they took the strange (or unholy) fire. I think if you were to take this account to any court of law, the judge would say, "This is the most stupid thing I have ever heard! It makes no sense; it is irrational, insane. What difference does it make?"

The source of the fire Aaron's sons used for the censing happened to be by their own convenient choice.

I am truly sad to say it, but this is what has happened to the Church at large. Years ago, in my journey, I found my heart and my head were in two completely different worlds. I had all the knowledge of God, but in my heart, He felt distant from me and unknown. When I looked around at those who worshiped Him, I couldn't find Him anywhere. I was out of my depth. I began to hunger, as it says in Psalm 42, "As the deer pants for the water brooks, so my soul pants for You, O God."[16] I wanted to know Him in real life-experience and understand the truth of who He is. I wanted to "partake of His divine nature."[17]

In many ways, our idea of Christianity has been ruined through culture and interpretations and the minds of men. It is a battle to fight our way through the oversaturation of head knowledge and go back to the ancient ways.

I think more than anyone else, the apostles and their followers explained to us and told us what the Church is all about. The traditions they established gave life to their faith, continuity, stability and permanence. The Church of 2,000 years has survived because of the apostles' doctrines and the Holy Traditions that the Church followed faithfully. In the midst of hundreds of false cults and extreme opposition, these two factors kept the Church safe. The train has two rails to run on. It did not derail. Today this is truer and more important as ever.

In saying all this, I am not implying that God's Word is not absolute—it is absolute, infallible and inerrant. Still, there is so much more to understanding the ways of God, who so desperately wants to be more real to us than any human being that we know.[18]

Remember, when Jesus walked on earth, He had to deal with the Pharisees. They were the creation of a small group of Jewish people some 160 years before Christ was born.[19] Their original purpose was to rescue people from loose living and idolatry. They saw themselves as the separated people. But by the time of Christ, they had become incredibly self-righteous and legalistic. As you know, they were eventually the ones who actually helped see to it that our Lord was crucified. Why? Their *own* interpretations of the Scripture became god to them, which replaced God Himself.

Jesus talked quite strongly to the Pharisees. He said, "You search the Scriptures, for in them you think you have eternal life; and these are they which testify of Me. But you are not willing to come to Me that you may have life" (St. John 5:39–40).

✝ ✝ ✝

Psychology tells us if somebody wants to do something, the most important element required is desire. To some, their desire is for making money. For others, it is physical pleasure. Then again for someone else, it could be cultivating a reputation for themselves.

If you are one called by Jesus and you want to be His follower, you, by your will, must choose to lay aside what *you* want, and your will, or desire, must be to do only what HE wants you to do—that's in all things. Whether you eat, drink or breathe, you do it all for His glory.[20] Following Christ and partaking of His nature is a life of absolute surrender.

The Bible says we are called to live as Jesus lived on earth.[21] But what does that mean for you and me on a practical, tangible level? This is more than a mental assent. For the Desert Fathers and Mothers, they chose to always have the mindset of abiding by the teachings of Christ, because His teachings are the only things that help us to stay one with Him.

Choosing to live by the church calendar seasons, such as Advent and Lent, and by the symbols of our faith, such as the sacrament of holy Baptism, becomes all important in our journey as the people of God. Notice how the Jewish people, no matter where they were in the world, for thousands of years lived *visibly* as the Jewish community. Embracing the sacramental life is the only way to keep our lives linked with the invisible God.

✠ ✠ ✠

In the early Church, the new Christian converts were mostly Jewish. On Sabbath (Saturday), they all went to the synagogues to listen to the Word read and to offer prayers. But on the Lord's Day (Sunday), these persecuted believers would gather together in homes for the breaking of bread.[22] They didn't come together on Sunday mornings for a speaker to give them a positive thought for the week. They gathered solemnly around the Holy Communion (Eucharist), to partake of His Holy Body and Holy Blood. And they would remember Jesus' words, "Unless you eat the flesh of the Son of Man and drink His blood, you have no life in you."[23]

As I write these chapters and talk about words and traditions like theosis or Eucharist, I understand that some of what I am saying may be unfamiliar or even uncomfortable. If you are seeking for the truth, I think you will eventually arrive at the reality that Holy Communion (the Eucharist) is an important, unexplainable mystery. It is the invisible, meeting with the visible—a tangible means of receiving God's grace. I pray that you will take time to think deeply about it. I myself have wished a thousand times that I had known these things when I was 20 or 25 years old. I am not trying to be a strange mystic or trying to say we should become legalistic by any means. I only wish to share what I've been learning on this journey of following the Lord these past many years.

One of the most encouraging things the Lord has said to me is, "Don't forget—you are still walking. At the end of your journey, I am going to be there, and you are going to meet Me."

In this life, we are called to live in the light of eternity, where "we shall always be with the Lord."[24] Our undistracted focus will be on Him, and on nothing and no one else. This type of worship is constant in the throne room of Heaven.[25] In the same manner, when you go to your local church, the primary reason is not to hear a guest preacher or listen to a wonderful music group. Your one overriding reason for going is to encounter God and to worship Him. It is God who invites His people to gather as one and worship Him. "Gather my people unto me."[26] "Unto Him shall the gathering of the people be."[27]

✝ ✝ ✝

Another question is worth asking: As the people of God, *what do we do when leaving a place of worship?*

Stated another way: *What is the result of us gathering to worship the living God and partake in the Holy Communion?*

We are sent out to be His witnesses. At the end of our Sunday services—after we've gathered together in worship, been taught from His Holy Word, confessed our sins together, received the Lord's forgiveness and partaken in His Holy Body and Blood—there is a benediction that the priest gives the congregation, which includes sending the people of God to *go* and be His living bold witness so that those that don't know Him will come to know the love of God.

In the Book of Acts, these new Christians began to be His witnesses, and they were persecuted, abused, but it says they "preached the Good News about Jesus wherever they went."[28] How quickly they seemed to be able do this! But it was an emphasis of the apostles. "Now you have new life," they were told, "wherever you go, talk about it."[29]

Jesus was radical. He gave up His will to do His Father's will. He lived for eternity. He embraced suffering. He didn't care about man's praise. He loved all people. He only sought the Father's glory. And Jesus told His followers, "You are the light of the world, you are the salt of the earth."[30]

A few years ago, some of our clergy learned that a forest-dwelling tribe living up in the hills not far from them were infected with severe malaria and dying. So, our people decided to make the journey, carrying with them several hundred mosquito nets and medicines as they climbed through the hilly terrain. It took them a whole day to get to the top of the forest where the tribe lived. When they arrived, they distributed the nets and showed the people how to use them, gave them medicines, but they didn't say a word about God or Jesus. They simply gave their gifts and went back home. When they trekked back a few months later to check on the people, they found everyone alive and well. Nobody else had died since receiving the mosquito nets and medicine! Grateful for these strangers' life-saving help, the tribe wanted to know *why* they had done such a kindness for strangers, and so the men shared with them about the love of Christ that compelled them. Now by God's grace there is a church among these people. This is just one example of the transforming power of Christ's love.

As the people of God, we have the responsibility and privilege to act on behalf of a world that is in such need of Jesus, who still weeps for and cares for it. Exercise love and compassion, especially toward those going through chaos in life. "Give, and it will be given to you" (St. Luke 6:38). The suffering we have lived through must be used by us so that we may be able to help others.[31] We learn and change and then become the means to help others.

Let me ask you, when was the last time you actively went out of your way to show the love of Christ to someone, and then to talk to them about His love for them? Jesus said that He "has come to seek and save that which was lost."[32] He sought out the suffering and the poor and showed them kindness. Can we say the same things about our own lives?

✝ ✝ ✝

What is the Great Commission? The Bible says that the words of Jesus were: "All authority has been given to Me in Heaven and on earth. Go therefore and make disciples of all the nations, baptizing them in the name of the Father and of the Son and of the Holy Spirit, teaching them to observe all things that I have commanded you; and lo, I am with you always, even to the end of the age" (St. Matthew 28:18–20).

I've noticed a sad trend taking place, where many now believe that doing social work is equal to fulfilling the Great Commission.

There was a time when I was a radical, calling for only preaching the Gospel and forgetting about any kind of social work. I've since had to repent and change my ways from saying social work cannot be mission work. I realized Jesus cared for the poor and needy, the hungry and the destitute, and He was moved by their suffering. Yes, God cares for them. You read that throughout the Old Testament as well. Some people say, "God destroyed Sodom and Gomorrah because of homosexuality." But in the book of Ezekiel you read that that's not all. God destroyed those cities because they did not extend justice in the way they treated the poor and the helpless, like the widows and orphans.[33]

Now I say, we as a Church, must do one hundred times more kind deeds to help the orphans and the sick and the suffering and the poor and the hungry throughout the world. But we should *not* assume that those deeds *alone* fulfill the Great Commission. Yes, we should minister to those who are hurting for one reason or another. But Jesus also saw people as sheep without a shepherd. They were helpless and tormented by demons and sin. People need the Lord. They are loved by God, and He wants them to be healed from their sins. How? —through the Holy Blood of Christ that was poured out for them.

I'm gripped by the story of Fr. Damien, a Catholic priest who left his home in Europe and went to one of the remote islands of Hawaii to which were banished all the people who had contracted leprosy. There were only one-way tickets to this island! There was no return. You could never come back to the mainland. And Fr. Damien went to the rulers of Hawaii and asked if he could go to the island of Molokai to serve the lepers.

They told him, "Father, once you go there, you cannot come back."

He said, "I know."

For over a dozen years, he worked among these people with leprosy—people who were considered as rejected, forsaken, unknown, undone and unforgiven. And he lived among them as someone who sees them and cares. He was the living Christ among them. And he used to pray, "Oh God, have mercy on these my brothers and sisters who have leprosy." Finally, he realized, he too had contracted the disease. His prayer changed: "Oh Lord, Heavenly Father, have mercy on *us* lepers." And he died there. No wonder he is known as St. Damien, the saint of lepers.[34]

✝ ✝ ✝

I'll never forget receiving information about two of our evangelists in a forbidden, or closed, country where they were not permitted to do visible mission work. They decided to walk three days through rough paths, through jungles, to get to *one* individual who had communicated with us, saying, "I heard on the radio about your God who loves me. This book you talk about, I never saw it." And these two dear evangelists from our Believers Eastern Church walked for three days, even after their feet began to bleed. But finally, when they got to this tiny village at the end of the country, they found this man on his mat, paralyzed, sick. They talked to him and explained about Christ and prayed for him, and Jesus Christ mercifully healed him. That was the beginning of a church in his community for that part of the world. So often it seems we live as though we don't believe "Jesus Christ is the same yesterday, today and forever."[35] But the Book of Acts is a blueprint for our time today to be His witnesses in word and deed.

Another story that touched me deeply was when I met a man in his 50s who was still strong and able to tell me his story. He told me, "I'm the man who persecuted your priest and beat him up and created every resistance I could to drive him out of the community." But one day, this man had an accident and broke his leg. Stuck in his hut, he was abandoned as all his friends who had helped him to attack our priest now left him. But our priest from the local congregation went to him and asked, "Can I help you?"

And our priest of the local parish carried him on his back to a place where he could hire a Jeep and take him to the hospital. The man didn't have the money to get the help he needed. So, our priest went from door to door, begging for money, so he could pay for treatment for his former enemy. When he was finally at the hospital and seen by doctors, his condition was so bad that they thought he would need to have his leg amputated. But with prayer and great care, although it took months of treatment and surgery—he was completely healed. Only minor scars were left on his heel. Later he came back to our priest and said these words, "I cannot resist your Jesus anymore." And today, he's one of the lay leaders in our local church!

✟ ✟ ✟

Well, I guess I've worked my way back to a hospital story. I believe that's where I started this chapter.

Hospitals deal with physical problems: broken bones, an infected appendix, a head wound, cancer, etc., and they have treatment plans for such afflictions. But a name board, no matter how prominent, declaring a building as a hospital doesn't make it a genuine place of healing. We found that out the hard way. Real hospitals don't distribute fake medicine.

Churches deal with matters of the spirit and soul: sin and forgiveness, spiritual life and death, holiness, etc. But a sign saying "church" doesn't make a given structure a genuine place of spiritual healing either—some people also find that out the hard way.

Common sense tells us that people would be wise to carefully choose the doctor or the hospital to which they entrust their lives. It should be even more obvious that it's even more important when they're thinking about a pastor or a church to which they entrust their souls.

Perhaps you've already noticed, we are living in the last minute of time. And I am deeply concerned about the apathy in the Church today. Getting a weekly dose of positive thinking in order to live happier lives on earth is not what we are called to. Rather, our lives must be intertwined with the life of God. Not just in a set of beliefs but visibly in our everyday life—in our sitting and our kneeling, in our words and our silence. When we labor with our hands to serve the poor, or we use them to make the sign of the cross. It is about Him, not us.

When it's all said and done, the day is soon coming when you will be alone, standing before God. Your spouse, your parents, your priest, your friends—they will not be there with you. It's only you and Him. I would ask you to really stop and think about that. That's all that I'm thinking about these days, all that matters anymore. I have a few more years left to be here on earth, and temporal distractions like material possessions, comfort, and a nice life hold no attraction for me. Rather, these things are overshadowed by my expectation and anticipation of the day when I will stand alone before the Lord.

Think about the God you worship—is He the real Jesus of the New Testament? Are the Bible teachings you've heard and the books you've read pointing you to the Christ who came to give His life for others? Do you sense a growing ache for those who do not know the love of Christ? Do you feel a deeper burden to care for the suffering and needy, lepers, widows and orphans as He did?[36]

One last question: Is your journey causing you to hunger even more to know God?

It is time to be free from our own selves and the enticements this world has to offer. I pray that you and I will continue to yield our lives and everything in us so that our actions and very thinking will be centered on the Lord.

Now is the greatest opportunity to do more for the needy and the hurting in our world; to set aside time and study the life of Christ and the apostles to learn how they worshiped; to go back to the beginning and see what we are missing. Why? Because there are only a few days left. Like the Scripture says, "Night is coming when no one can work."[37]

With your prayers, your time, your giving, your very life, my challenge is this: Think deeply about your life and purpose. Return to the true living God. Remember His longing for His creation—and the sacrifices He made. Meditate on His Word, not for the brilliant doctrines you might discover, but to learn His heart and become like Him.

The start of your *new* journey can be now.

✟ ✟ ✟

The battle is wearisome, and it's normal to want to quit. But when we realize that we have come a long way and when we feel His presence, strength and grace, that will see us through, our hearts will be encouraged not to give up. We must remain focused. This is the lesson I am learning; I have a long way to go. But the long way is not endless . . . . The signs are no longer covered by fog. Just a few more turns, and we will cross the finish line. The end has begun. We will talk about it in the next chapter. Let us long to finish well.

This is the beginning of the end. Hang on.

CHAPTER EIGHT

BEGINNING OF THE END

Time shall no more be.

— Revelation 10:6[1]

I first went to the United States in 1974 to go to college. It was a new world to me with all kinds of fascinating things. In the house where I lived, there was a black-and-white television set, and it was on most of the time. The star of a show I liked was a man who to me looked a lot like Gandhiji with his little round glasses. His name was George Burns, and he was a comic. He always had a long cigar, and I thought he was quite funny. Before his show ended, he would always sing this song, "I wish I was 18 again."[2] Well, his wish didn't come true. Even though Burns lived to be quite old, he never was 18 again before he died.

I, too, kind of wish I could be 18 again, especially if I could know all the things I now know. That won't happen for any of us.[3]

This reminds me of a close friend whose journey has been like mine. He's written a number of books and has served God in several capacities. There came a time in his life when he had what you might call a midlife crisis. He suddenly realized that, despite all the knowledge and experience he had gained, and the success he'd known in his ministry, there was still a great emptiness inside him. This longing was something his theological degrees from the seminary hadn't satisfied.

He decided to cut back on his hectic schedule and spend more time alone with the Lord. Not just minutes or hours, but days, in silence, solitude; meditating on the Word to know God.

One day he had what must have been a vision. He said it was like someone came to him wearing a white robe. "Come with me," he was told. Almost immediately my friend sensed it was Christ, so he responded, "Where are we going, Lord?" The only answer was, "Come."

The two walked together through a beautiful green meadow and then up rolling hills and finally they came to a plateau at the top of an outcropping. That's when the Lord spoke once again.

"Look straight ahead and tell Me what you see."

They were looking at a sunset with the sun just starting to disappear over the horizon. Before he had time to respond, he heard Christ say to him, "My son, only a few days left, get to know me." And he disappeared.

My friend came back to his senses realizing that however long he had to live, his time would be all too short. His life was turned upside-down. Instead of running around doing a thousand different things in the world, he needed to put more value on quietness and solitude, making sure he was always living the will of his Heavenly Father. Being able to say yes or no depending on the precise desires of God, even as *Jesus* did when here on the earth[4] was now his foremost purpose, and he was forever changed.

Today, I am still radical in my commitment to bring the love of Christ to those who haven't heard the Good News of the love their Heavenly Father has for them. Nothing has changed in that regard. But I have also discovered the joy of intimacy with Him. That now comes first for me. I am also aware that my journey here on earth will end all too soon. I can no longer afford to spend time on self-chosen projects, or efforts that the Lord doesn't regard as top priorities. And I won't know what those are if I'm not walking close to Him.

In C.S. Lewis's *Narnia* series, there is a passage called "The Final Word from Aslan." (As a reminder, Aslan is the great lion who is a Christ figure.) There he says, "Here on the mountain the air is clear, and your mind is clear; as you drop down into Narnia, the air will thicken. Take great care that it does not confuse your mind. And the Signs which you have learned here will not look at all as you expect them to look, when you meet them there."[5]

This world is not our home. Its ways are not the ways of Heaven. For whatever reason, that's not an easy lesson to learn. I'm grateful that C.S. Lewis makes this a major point as he writes his *Narnia* series with children in mind.

For that matter, what 18-year-old young adult has mastered such a lesson? My guess is that there are few indeed. So, who wants to be 18 again? Maybe 28 or 38 would be a better option. Should we make it 48 or 58? Unfortunately, *I wish I was 58 again* doesn't sound like all that catchy a song title.

How good it is that in the life to come, our learning won't have to be crammed into several decades or so!

✢ ✢ ✢

I remember an all-night prayer meeting in India a while back. There must have been no less than a thousand attendees, probably more. Right after the midnight break, we regrouped for a session when individuals could voice their private prayers.

A woman started praying. It was obvious her prayer was being said with a tremendous amount of emotion and tears, and I was terribly curious to see who this person was. I opened my eyes to look around and realized she was an old woman on her knees with arms raised and her face turned toward Heaven. Her head was covered with a prayer shawl, and the words she cried out in her prayer went something like this:

"Lord Jesus, I have loved You all my life. I've waited and waited for You to come back. It has been so long, and the journey is so long and hard. Please, Lord, when will You come back? How much longer must I wait before I can see You face to face? Please come back soon."

Maybe she forgot all the people sitting around her while she was lost in that prayer. The only thing that seemed to be on her mind was her great longing to see the Lord face to face.

The following day I inquired about her, and I was told that as a young woman studying in college, she had given her life to Christ. Upon hearing of this, her family members had disowned her. She had to walk away from all she had known, with only the clothes she was wearing. All her life she remained single, and her commitment was to pray and to share with others how much she loved Jesus and who He is.

When I saw her at that meeting, she must have been 80 or maybe even 90-odd years old. I wish now that I had asked her, "Dear woman, what keeps you going?" Obviously, having faced rejection from her family, losing whatever inheritance and support she might have had, never marrying or having a family, not following after the typical aspirations people have—all of these things must have been very difficult for her. Would she wish for the chance to be 18 again?

I imagine she would have replied something like this: "You know, all I want is to see Him. I know everything in this world will eventually burn. The only thing that remains is the reality of our Lord Jesus Christ and the Holy Trinity, and I live only for Him. I look forward to the day at the end of my journey when at last I can see Him face to face. The Scripture says when I see Him, I shall be like Him.[6] He will wipe away all the tears from my eyes. That longing, that knowledge, helps me move forward despite the difficulties and the aloneness I often feel."

People like this make us take stock of our lives here on earth. A man may be a multi-billionaire, he may have all the property deeds and business certificates and all such things, but sooner or later he will die. The medical doctor who treats his patients will die, and all of his patients will, too. This is the ending of the story of all humans! Yours too!

As a matter of fact, recently I was with someone who told me about one of the few millionaires who lived not far from us. When I was in college, I knew of him. Anyway, he is dead now, and the truth is that he couldn't take even a penny of that fortune with him into the next world. He had to leave everything to his children, who one day will also die. Well, I didn't say anything further in the conversation, but as I think about these matters, given a choice between the two, I believe I would rather live like the old woman did and become old like her, loving and longing for her Lord.

✠ ✠ ✠

Too often we forget that we are here for only a short time. All those God has elected to be His are left here on earth as spiritual children to go through the school of life to learn God's ways. The few years we have down here are a training session in which we are equipped to reign with the Lord forever. When we make the decision that *Jesus, You are my Lord,* a transformation soon begins to take place. This individual, if he or she lives a sacramental life (a life fully set apart for the Lord), will see the importance of eternity and surrender to the Lord in every matter.

This incredible reality means we get to share in the beautiful way God begins to make Himself known through our earthen vessels, even as we experience a little of what it will be like to reign with Him for all eternity.

When here on earth we lose sight of this commitment, we start to meander. Consider the people who go to buy groceries with a list made out. They know exactly which store they are going to and which aisles and shelves they'll find the items on that they want. There is no meandering; their lives are intentional, focused.

By way of contrast, there are folks who just kind of walk around exploring, seeing if there might be something they hadn't thought about or might have missed. If they appear a little lost, a store employee might ask, "Is there something I can help you with?"

"Oh, no," they answer, "I'm just looking around."

It's like this is a hobby. They might buy nothing, or they might buy things on impulse that they later regret. They have no intention to get something done and be on their way. This is the kind of life a lot of people live, even those who claim to be Christians.

I thank God daily for His mercy in holding my hand and letting me continue to walk with Him and never allowing me to walk away, although there have been more than enough attempts by *me* to do so. His grace and His mercy have kept me from wandering away.

This is what happens when we are able to be alone and understand the ways of God. It is the journey I began to understand when I started studying the early Church. All of a sudden, you find you are being set free from the things all around you and realize that life here is not everything; this is all going to end.

What can give us the motivation to press on amid so many distractions surrounding us? It is the awareness that time is very short, and we simply cannot afford to give our lives to the things of this world.

✛ ✛ ✛

In Acts 20, we find the Apostle Paul saying goodbye to the leaders of the church in Ephesus. He says something like this, "Look, I have been with you all these years. I don't have much of anything, just these clothes on my back. That's about it. I preached day and night, and God used me to minister to you. I worked with my own hands to make money to pay for my food and travel, for myself and my friends. I didn't even take a penny from anyone. And yes, I know what's ahead . . . persecution, beatings, even losing my life. But then, I don't regard my life as dear to myself."[7]

In other words, he was doing exactly what our Lord said in St. Matthew and St. John: "I am sending you out as sheep among wolves.[8] Yes, you will have problems, but I will be with you."[9]

These last few years for me have been like surviving in a maze of pain. You already read how, during horrendous emotional grief, I even considered taking my life. This made me feel great shame, but then I realized that there is in me, as a human being, still a bit of love for my life. Even so, I'll never forget kneeling beside my bed there in the Metropolitan's house before dawn and saying, "Jesus, I don't think there is anyone else in this place, just me and You, and I really need to talk. There are a couple of security guards out there, I guess, to make sure no one can get in and try to kill me. All that really has no meaning, does it? Anyway, what I want to say to You is that I began this journey as a young man of only 17 years of age. I was just skin and bones, and I knelt back then beside a bed far from my home, and I remember saying to You that I didn't have any money, or popularity, or a degree, or much of anything. All I had was a fragile little body, but if You wanted it, it was Yours. And I gave myself to You.

"Now, some five decades later, I've ended up back at pretty much that same place. But my prayer has changed. I can hardly wait for the day this journey ends and I can see You face to face. Eternity with You really sounds good to me. No beginning or ending—a perpetual present. Living in a place beyond time! Everlasting . . . infinite!

"Well, I again choose to lay down my life for You, Lord. In fact, if I were to be given the privilege of being a martyr, that would be a great honor. Truth be told, I am no more intent on living for myself. I am dead. Thank you for listening to this broken vessel . . . Amen."

I seek no sympathy. I seek only to share the struggle of this one little, fragile human being through this earthly pilgrimage. What keeps me going is what kept so many in those early centuries of the Church moving on, despite what they faced. All those godly men and women, who we now call saints, chose to walk fear-lessly with their heads held high, even into the arena to be killed by lions or swords or whatever else.

Listen to me. If you are more concerned about your house or car or furniture or reputation or friends or future or any of the things of this world that can grab people's attention while they are passing through this life, you have a way to go as a follower of Christ. Remember that the higher we climb, the clearer the air and the greater the ability to recognize beauty. The more we bury ourselves in the world and its noise, the less we understand God's timeless perspective.[10] Always remember, wise Christians determine to live their lives in the light of eternity.

In our journey as part of the Holy Church, and even in my own life, we have been through more than we ever imagined in terms of what the world has thrown at us. Even the best of Christian leaders, we've learned, can simply turn away and, in the end, you find yourself alone, limping through the wilderness. This is where you hear Him saying, "You are not alone. I am with you. I will never leave you or forsake you."[11]

But He will take away all the crutches you depend on, one by one, even if that crutch is ministry and serving Him. I came to the place where I had to realize

I *don't own* anything. The ministry I am part of is not mine, it's the Lord's. I understand a little better what St. Paul said, "Having received this work, this ministry from the Lord, we do not give up."[12]

I've been tempted to walk away from the Lord more times than you can imagine. But, again and again, I have to come to the place where I say, I am a struggling human being, but thank God for people like St. Paul and St. Polycarp and others who went before me in the days of old. I can look to them and know I still have a long, long way to go. And I say, "Oh Lord, have mercy on me, a sinner."

☩ ☩ ☩

Recently I had the privilege to go to Myanmar to visit with our Archdioceses and, of course, speak to all our priests, evangelists and church workers there. By the grace of God, Believers Eastern Church has more than 400 strong, local parishes in this nation. These parishes reach out to serve three neighboring countries where they have already started a number of churches. In talking to the Archbishop, he reminded me of the history of his country, Myanmar, or what was earlier called Burma.

He recounted for me once again the life of Adoniram Judson and his wife. This couple came and laid down their lives to share the Gospel. That was despite endless suffering, persecution and death.

Adoniram and his family left his home country, America, to serve the poor and needy in Myanmar (Burma) in early 1900s. It would take months of tedious journey to get to this new country where the unknown awaited them.

His wife, Nancy, was born and raised in a very wealthy home, yet she was willing to give up everything to follow Christ with her husband to Burma.

The Judsons worked hard for seven years before even one person believed in Christ. It took many more years before they had 18 people meeting for worship.

Their first boy died during their voyage from Calcutta (Kolkota) to Burma. The second baby, Roger, died before reaching his ninth month.

Adoniram faced much persecution and was imprisoned for nearly 20 months. He was tortured without mercy by religious fundamentalists. One night, his bleeding feet were hanging in elevated stocks and swarms of mosquitos settled on his bare soles, causing unbearable pain and agony.

Shortly after his release from prison, his dear wife, Nancy, died. The suffering and sacrifice borne alone in a strange culture took its toll. Then within a few weeks, their little daughter Maria, their third baby, also died without any warning.

Adoniram was left all alone in a hostile land, full of pain, grief and fear.

A lot of people who'd gone to help him left, for they could not stand the inconvenience and difficulties of the mission field.

He had before him only jungles, with wild and dangerous animals and swarms of killer mosquitos, and he was forsaken by all he had thought would be his friends.

But in spite of all the loss and suffering he faced, he did not give up his work. He reasoned to himself, if he did not pay the price to bring the love of God to these people, who would?

Adoniram's radical commitment to Christ was not in vain. Today, there are several million Christians in Myanmar, and the leaders like our Archbishop credit all this to the Judsons, who were true pioneers, spending their lives to bring Christ's love to this nation.

More recently, it was the missionary Jim Elliot, one of five young, martyred missionaries down in Ecuador's rainforest, who wrote the following at the age of only

22: "He is no fool who gives what he cannot keep to gain what he cannot lose."[13]

✝ ✝ ✝

Let me leave you with this request. Please learn to live your life, every minute of it, in the light of eternity. A day will come when all your family, friends, responsibilities, possessions, degrees, popularity, all of it will be gone. It's just going to be you and Christ and nothing else. Let the decisions you make today be ones that will reflect well in the light of that moment.

There will be trials, just like Job faced, and you'll see how much your faith can stand. This is God's pruning, and He will allow it countless times. Throughout this process, our character will become more and more Christ-like, and we will gain a deeper understanding of His Word. We will no longer be the kind of person we were five or 10 years ago. I recently read a book on Job's life published by Vintage Books, and it helped me understand the mystery behind the trials and suffering we face in life, allowed by God.[14]

Through this pruning, God is then able to entrust us with greater responsibilities and more fruit. When this happens, God in His mercy will give us the support we need to carry on. But God's support in these times is not joy, peace, acclamation or the applause of men we might hope to receive. It is instead pain, trials and difficulties—something God chooses in His wisdom to keep us from getting proud and being unable to support the weight of the fruit He gives us.

Although these tests and trials are sure to come, keep in mind that Jesus never said: "Ok, come here, put this cross on and carry it now." No, the choice to do that is ours. He said, "If anyone *wants* to come after Me, let him deny himself and take up his cross and follow Me daily."[15] No compulsion. No beating you up to do this or that. It is a loving choice you make because your greatest longing is to see Him—the One who loved you enough to die for you.

It is worth living for Him, and if the privilege is given, to die for Him.

Never forget His unchanging promise. As we take the yoke upon us, HE is on the other side, carrying the burden along with us.[16] We are never alone.

Make all decisions in the light of eternity. Know that even the forest fires we walk through now will dim to nothing in that light.

✠ ✠ ✠

In India, we travel a lot by train. It can be jam-packed with not an inch to move. As we get to the next station or our destination, we will know it even if we don't know the route because people will start shoving and moving like the tide towards the door—it is time to get off. So it is with our life journey on earth. It is almost time to go home. He is even at the door. The next chapter, *One Minute to Midnight,* will make you glad that this journey of pain and suffering is not long!

This is the shadow land! Don't put down deep roots in this world.

CHAPTER NINE

ONE MINUTE TO MIDNIGHT

*Precisely because we cannot predict the moment,
we must be ready at all moments.*

— C.S. Lewis [1]

I have never really liked traveling all that much. Years ago I thought, *when I reach the age of 60, I will stop these endless trips and stay in one place for a while.* But it looks like that wish remains on hold. Just as I've been working on this chapter, I arrived in Delhi again. I had a dinner meeting scheduled with one of the Ambassadors from an African nation and the Archbishop of the Anglican church of his country, along with our own Archbishop from our Delhi Archdiocese. This meeting will help propel our dream of expanding to Africa in the near future, God willing. I was, and still am, grateful that this urgency is felt by our Episcopal Synod (College of Bishops).

When our ministry first started in 1979, all I knew was non-stop travel in the West, and at least seven or eight times a year back to Southeast Asia. In those days you could buy an air pass for a few hundred dollars to travel for 30 or 60 days. I can't even count how many times my wife, Gisela, and my little children drove me to the airport to catch my next flight. I would see them again after three or four weeks. I was going from meeting to meeting, pouring my heart out for the untold multitudes in various nations who needed to hear about the love of Christ.

I don't have many regrets in my life, but I do have a few. I feel sad about how I was gone from home so much, leaving my young wife, Gisela (we were in our twenties), and our two children for the sake of sharing about the needs of the broken and hurting world. I feel a great deal of grief and have often cried about those painful years when *she* had to raise our children without their father and her husband. I am troubled even now when I reflect on it. I have cried alone often thinking about the suffering my dear wife and children went through! It is a truth I must face.

I remember, so often, when they took me to the airport, my little daughter, Sarah, and my young son, Daniel, cried their eyes out asking for their daddy not to go. But Gisela never shed a tear; she kept her composure.

Later, I learned, after the three got back home, she would go to our bedroom, close the door and weep by herself. It wasn't just the children who missed me!

When my two little ones would ask if their daddy was coming back soon, she would never complain or be negative. Rather, she would hold them close and say things like, "If we didn't let Daddy go to speak in these meetings, so many people in our world would not hear about God's love. He is able to do that because we three are willing to sacrifice our rights for the sake of Christ and people in great need, who are poor and desperate."

Another regret is that I wish I had been kinder and more loving to others. I have cried dozens of times thinking of the many incidents of my impatience and unloving attitude to the brothers and sisters around me in the body of Christ. I have had to ask forgiveness from many. I now pray over and over each day, "Lord Jesus Christ, Son of God, have mercy on me a sinner." More often than I am sure I even realize, in the midst of seeing the needs of so many without names around the world whom I am compelled to help, I often miss seeing the needs of those sitting right in front of me.

The older I get, the weaker I feel, and the more often I find myself failing. I know there is still a long way to go to be like my Lord. But I must go on, knowing our God is a God of mercy and love.

Love and kindness are the litmus tests of our knowledge of Christ. I am grateful for my understanding of theosis that has transformed my life, especially over these last few years, to the extent that I hardly recognize myself and the way my heart and mind now respond to people. I truly can say I have no enemies, for you can only truly have enemies when you have enmity in your heart. Today, all I have is a deep love and longing for all to know Him and love Him.

I feel sad, too, regarding the many years I spent serving God but did not think about the poor and the suffering in our world. I had to repent and change my ways and even add what was a new chapter to my book *Revolution in World Missions.*[2] That addition was about caring especially for children without hope, who are found on the streets of many nations. Later I wrote a book about it, called *No Longer a Slumdog!*[3]

Even the things that we look back and wish we could have handled differently, even those things, God takes them and He mends them and does something new through them. One of the best things Gisela and I did in our early years was to take our little children every year to Asian nations, so that they understood truth beyond the circumstances of their lives; developed true empathy for those who suffered and a deep appreciation of their duty to those people. This had a huge impact on them as they grew up in the West.

I'm so grateful when I think about my children, who are now married, have children of their own and have given us seven wonderful grandchildren. Both of them and their families not only know the Lord but serve Him as well.

Someone asked me what I consider to be among the greatest accomplishments in my life. This one person mentioned the number of books I had written, and that I am now the Metropolitan of Believers Eastern Church, and the radio broadcasts I have done, and so on. Without having to think I replied, "All I have done, anyone can do. To me, the most important thing is that I have two children, and both of them know the Lord, and with their families, they love Him and serve Him. This is my greatest accomplishment."

My son studied at our Major Seminary in India and then went on to Nepal to work with our Mission. His wife also spent a year or so in Nepal serving God after her seminary studies. Now they serve the Lord with us.

My daughter married a godly young man who is a medical doctor and also one of our priests. They both serve with our church in the Asian subcontinent.

Other than my own mother, who is now with Jesus, I can't think of anyone who knows the Lord as intimately as does my wife, Gisela. Just like my mother,

Gisela's favorite Bible verse is Psalm 73:25, "Whom have I in Heaven but you? And there is none upon earth that I desire besides you." We have been married for more than 45 years. Our desire is to walk with the Lord with the same commitment and call we received back when we were in our early 20s. It was then that we made a covenant to God, that Jesus would be more important to us than anything in the world, even each other. In this long journey of almost five decades of wonderful time together, this covenant remains true of us.

We believe that early on, our book *Revolution in World Missions* truly changed the mission world, and to us that is nothing short of a miracle. I've heard of no less than 60 mission organizations that were started all over the world as a result of it. That is the number we know about, and there may well be many more we will never know of. The fact is, you cannot have five million copies of this book in print, and in 12 different languages, without having a radical impact on the mission world. We give all the glory to God, for it is His doing.

Gisela and I have given our all for His sake. Our basic needs have always been met, and we live as simply as we can so that more people can come to know our wonderful Lord.

✝ ✝ ✝

In the first chapter of this book, I talked about my trip to India and that dark night of my soul that drove me close to suicide. But this flight to Delhi is quite different from that one. Now the lawsuit in the United States is over, and by God's grace, that is all resolved. We did not lose our faith, though we were severely tested,[4] and we continue to serve the Lord.

Now, as we come to almost the end of this journey, I do want to tell you one very important fact that we did not know at the beginning of our crisis. It all began with our wanting to become the community of Christ.

Moving from the city of Dallas, Texas, to the 700-acre rural setting was a real challenge.

You may ask, "Why was it so hard?"

Think about this: Abraham did not have to face the endless struggles, fear, grief and trials until he moved out from where he was to become a nation,[5] to be the means for God to create the people of God, or stated another way, the community of God.

The children of Israel didn't have to face the onslaught of the enemy within and without until they left Egypt to become the worshiping community of God.[6]

The prophet Jeremiah wouldn't have had to suffer for 40 years if he hadn't got involved with the people of God.[7]

So, what is it they have in common?

You see, when we understand the mystery of the community of God and choose to get involved in the center of His eternal plan, the enemy gets really upset. A loving and united community of Christ is the biggest threat to Satan. He does all he can to kill it before it takes shape, and if he can't kill it, he tries to cause as much crisis as possible to hurt the life of the community.

Take a look around. It's not hard to see that times are changing. Nothing will be the same again. The end is nearer than we think. We could even be the last generation!

Deep down in our hearts, we know the world will not and cannot go on forever as it is. Our challenge is to *flee* the world and all its lusts, and so be His holy people in this wicked and perverse generation.

Turn on the news and see the continual reports of tragic events taking place around the world. When you read the Bible, you understand that what we see around us now has already been predicted and that these are the signs that point to the end times.

I strongly encourage you to read the Gospels where the Lord Jesus talks about the signs of His second coming.

What God said will take place is happening.

We are told to give close attention and be diligent in living for the Lord, knowing this world will not be here for long. "And so we have the prophetic word confirmed, which you do well to heed as a light that shines in a dark place, until the day dawns and the morning star rises in your hearts; knowing this first, that no prophecy of Scripture is of any private interpretation, for prophecy never came by the will of man, but holy men of God spoke as they were moved by the Holy Spirit."[8]

Christ's second coming is *not* going to be some secret event without the knowledge of the world. He is coming to establish His kingdom in the city of Jerusalem, to rule the world. The early Fathers of the Church, as well as the ancient Christians, believed this and looked for it to happen.[9]

✝ ✝ ✝

To survive the onslaught of the enemy and hold on to our faith, even if it means persecution and death,[10] our hope is to learn to function as Christ's community,[11] and to stick together as it was in the beginning of the Church for those early Christians.

The world has seen violence, lawlessness and wars in every nation in every generation, but nothing has happened in history that can compare with what we've witnessed during these last 100 years or so. The wars and rumors of wars are increasing so rapidly, escalating every day.[12] There seems to be hardly one nation in the world that is not involved directly or indirectly in some kind of war.

The Bible says that if these days at the end of time were not shortened, even the elect of God would not survive them.[13] Plagues, diseases and epidemics have become so common today that words like Ebola and AIDS hardly give us reason to even pause. Humanity is overcome by thousands of unnamed diseases, and there seems to be no answer to the crisis of health care in our world.[14]

Our life here on earth, even with the best of health and circumstances, is only for a very short time compared to eternity. The ancient Church, it seems, continually reminded the followers of Christ to live their lives in the light of Christ's return.[15] What does that look like? It means for us to live as light in this dark and dying world.

The reason we are even more desperate to share the love of God to the ends of the earth today is because we believe what Jesus said in the Gospel of St. Matthew 24:3–8 about the signs of the end times, and we must obey Him.

I ask you to spend more time learning of the Lord's coming back. This will help give you the strength and motivation needed to face any trouble or suffering that might arise in the days to come in your journey with the Lord.

The Scripture very clearly says the last days are going to be like the days of Noah: "For as in the days before the flood, they were eating and drinking, marrying and giving in marriage, until the day that Noah entered the ark, and did not know until the flood came and took them all away, so also will the coming of the Son of Man be" (St. Matthew 24:38–39).

So, Christ clearly spelled out the signs of His coming and the end of the age, and He told us to be on the watch. This means that we must keep this truth about the return of Jesus always in mind. Don't let it get shoved way down the list, pretty much out of your daily thinking.

Here's a thought with which to wrestle. Ask yourself: "I believe in the return of Christ, but does it affect in any way how I live?" It's not an easy question to consider.

✝ ✝ ✝

The enemy also knows the night is nearly upon us, and he is more desperate than ever to stop the work of God by any means possible.[16] Our story is just one example of what can and will happen to those seeking to follow and obey Christ in our world today.

The admonition to us, upon whom the end of the world has come, is to "escape to the mountains."[17] The mountain is the hill of Golgotha, where you see the cross on which the Son of God was crucified.

This is the context from which for the last 15 years or more, I have been crying out, that we must *flee* from this noise of the world and become Christ's community and live according to the values of the early Church.

Not too long ago, I read a book called *The Benedict Option* by Rod Dreher. This book is a call for our modern Christianity to realize the need of living in Christ-centered communities if we are to make it through these final days.[18] He says, "If we want to survive, we have to return to the roots of our faith, both in thought and in practice. We are going to have to learn habits of the heart forgotten . . . . We are going to have to change our lives, and our approach to life, in radical ways. In short, *we are going to have to be the Church,* without compromise, no matter what it costs."[19]

What does it mean to be a Community of Christ?

For the early Church, the believers' lives revolved around worship, always living in close proximity (usually just walking distance) to the place where they gathered for worship. The Jewish community still does it this way.

The followers of Christ in the early centuries were small groups of people, usually 20–60 or so, meeting together in homes, worshiping and celebrating the Holy Communion.

The purpose of these communities is *not* for them to exist solely for themselves, but for them to be a place where Christ is at the center and where His life is able to flow freely among them to do His will. It is a source out of which missions flow.

One of our dreams after moving out to this campus in East Texas was to make a place for 100–200 young people to spend a year with us, to begin their spiritual journey in knowing the Lord and then be sent out to the whole world as His living witnesses. By faith, we will see a community of believers gathering from around the world to worship Christ, just like what can be found at the Taizé community in France.[20] From our community, individuals will be transformed to serve the whole Church.

We have had dozens of testimonies of transformation from young people who have been with us and had their lives completely turned around, and who are now alight for God after spending one year in our community. My prayer is to see thousands of young people go through our program in the coming years. This investment in young people has proven to be one of the most effective things we can do to help young people to be true disciples of the Lord. It is happening.[21]

One of my dreams is to see at least half a million children find hope through our ministry of helping the poor and needy children in our generation. I also live with the dream of seeing tens of thousands of worshiping communities among people who had never heard His name, spreading love and meaning to all people regardless of caste, creed, color, wealth or poverty.

These dreams and prayers of mine are reminders that there is still much to do before the Lord returns.

When I think of the Church today, I picture in my mind a clock like the clock in Times Square, New York City, only this clock is counting down to the end of the world. It shows one minute to midnight. Time is running out, and we can no longer afford not to act. It is later than we think.

✝ ✝ ✝

You have traveled with me through nine chapters, and hopefully it has been helpful in your journey with the Lord. With all our learning, changes, grooming, transformation—we still sometimes find ourselves so alone in silence. But it is within that silence when the Lord shows up, and we remember we are His creation, the clay in His hands. And that is all we need. He is everything we ever long for. I titled the final chapter of this book *Silence* with a specific purpose. And you will see why.

Find yourself, in silence with God.

CHAPTER TEN

SILENCE

Silence is a gift of God, to let us speak more intimately with God.

— St. Vincent Pallotti [1]

O ne of the more familiar memories from my final year in high school is the sound of about 38 students, all nearing adulthood, talking, shouting and whispering all at once. It might've been a classroom, yet it sounded like a marketplace! Noise, noise, noise. Words, words, words! Usually it happened during the first period.

All of a sudden, our class teacher would walk in, glance at the room full of chattering young people, raise his voice and say just one word: "Silence!" Instantly, a hush would descend over the entire classroom.

Pin drop silence.

Yet, knowing my classmates, I know that just like me, they were still talking within the sound of silence—chattering to themselves in their mind.

The silence in my classroom was forced upon us. We had no choice.

In the United States, you might hear someone say, "In accordance with my 5th Amendment rights, I choose to remain silent." Such a statement brings to mind movies in which a mafia member, when put on trial, refuses to testify for fear he might incriminate himself. Silence in such a setting strongly implies guilt.

This certainly wasn't the case, however, during the infamous trial of the Lord Jesus Christ. When brought before Herod, Pilate, the religious hierarchy and the crowd with its bloodthirst awakened, it surely cannot have been easy for this Almighty God in flesh to be ridiculed and mocked without responding, especially when He could have immediately drawn on more than enough power to free himself and punish everybody who wished Him harm if He had simply desired to do so.

There is an emotionally moving picture hanging in my study. The picture is of Christ being questioned by Pilate, and from the body language one can see, feel... silence—Christ's only response.

How often have I sat on the floor in silence, leaning against the wall, gazing at this picture! Somehow, I find myself being transported back in time, standing somewhere in that room, transfixed by the mystery of silence beyond silence I see on Christ's face!

I often remind myself of the sign of our Lord's incredible strength and resolve by remaining so close-mouthed. It makes me think of the Old Testament, Messianic passage, "He was oppressed and He was afflicted, yet He opened not His mouth; He was led as a lamb to the slaughter, and as a sheep before its shearers is silent, so He opened not His mouth" (Isaiah. 53:7).

Looking back over the five decades of my journey in serving God, one of the most difficult disciplines I encountered was the discipline of silence. It has only been during these years of my inner hunger to know God and live before Him that I have realized the importance of silence and solitude. I must yield myself to experience the reality of knowing God. The early Church Fathers and others were great participants of this practice, and I was deeply challenged by their examples.

One of the biggest problems right now for many is that they are running and running, with little sense of God, and they can't shut off all the noise around them because they think noise keeps them sane. But once we withdraw for a day or two of silence with Him, we find we have entered a whole different world. I believe God waits for us to purposely draw apart from this world of noise and busyness to experience more of His presence![2]

Maybe you are even busy doing God's work much of the time. I fear a lot of what we do is often performance, with little of it being empowered by God. This busyness could all be burned up one day[3] because the only thing that lasts in eternity is what was created through the energy and the life of God functioning through our earthen vessels. That's why St. Paul confessed that, as a human being, nothing of spiritual value could be the result of his own soulish work. And by *soulish* I mean what is born out of our flesh instead of the Spirit of God.[4] All that is of God can only originate with God. This is an important lesson, one I think lots of us need to learn, especially those of us in the work of God.

I fear too many Christians today hardly know the difference between the Church and the world anymore. But as for me, I hear a voice, sometimes distant, but clear and loud saying, "Come away, My love. Come away, be Mine."

Keith Green, who is now alive with the Lord, was a dear friend. He wrote a song[5] using those words I just quoted above, and they still speak powerfully to me. I must never get so active doing the Lord's business that I don't set aside quality time with Him.

The Bible has plenty of examples to tell us this truth that demonstrate the importance of this time alone with the Lord. John the Baptist lived in the wilderness;[6] the Apostle Paul spent three years in the Arabian Desert before going into ministry; even Jesus spent 40 days alone fasting and praying before He began His public ministry.[7] Once that started, we still find Him regularly escaping the crowds, and sometimes even His disciples, to ensure that He had long hours alone with His Father.[8] As I mentioned before, it seems our Lord's life was marked by few words, and silence, even in the final hours of His journey on earth. In my flesh, I don't like to be alone, but being with the Invisible and being silent before Him is a different thing. Nothing is more peaceful than listening to the Lord in silence.

✝ ✝ ✝

There is another angle to this concept of silence that I want to briefly explore before closing. When we look at Jesus during His final week on earth, the consistent picture we get is one of our Lord purposely remaining almost mute. It's as though He had reasoned that nothing He said would change what would happen. The crowd had made up their mind to crucify Him. These people had already determined His fate; further comments from Him would not alter the direction in which things were going, so why waste words!

These observations about Jesus and this matter of silence were helpful for me to ponder when reports in the media raised accusations against me regarding financial matters. Could it be that silence was the most Christ-like response?

Looking back, I wish I could report that a most-meaningful prayer time had resolved the issue once and for all for me. I imagine it could have taken place in our church, the St. Peter's Believers Eastern Church in our community at Wills Point. You step through the massive wooden door and into this beautiful church, and you feel like you have walked into the very presence of God. The century-old stained glass with icons of spiritual realities, the high ceiling, the altar area, the absolute quietness that makes one not even whisper... you kneel and pray. I picture it as a beautiful evening, the weather perfect, and I say to the Lord:

"This experience I have been going through has been very difficult, Lord. Never before have I been falsely accused like this, and in such a public way. Maybe now I understand a little better, anyway, of what Your suffering was like that final week of Your life. I am so sorry You were treated the way You were.

"As You know, God, these articles about me are all lies. They have made me angry and determined to defend myself. What that latest blogger wrote is not at all who I am!"

I pause, listening.

"What's that?

"No... no police or military figure mocked me or hurt me in any way.

"There was no unusual nighttime interrogation.

"Uh-uh, I wasn't handcuffed or bound in some fashion. Yes, I'm truly thankful for that.

"Spat at? No.

"Not socked in the face, either.

"Slapped, no.

"The people who accused me didn't organize a mob thirsty for my blood and death.

"I wasn't flogged or physically beaten in any way.

"I'm still alive, yes."

Dear reader, that is what I imagine the scene would have been like, the one I wish I had had, the one I imagined, but the one that never came to be. I wish I could report that that was what happened. But still, I picture how the rest of it might have followed.

If I had continued in this fashion, I probably needed to say:

"Don't answer, Jesus, but this trial I've gone through was undoubtedly much easier than what many of those in the early Church experienced, right?

"And in Your vast Church around the world, especially in places where Christians are decidedly in the minority, I have to assume that some of Your own are facing situations right now that are far worse than what I am presently going through, correct?

"You are incredibly good, God, and I love You very much. Thank You for listening and allowing me to tell You what has been tumbling around in my head. I think I'll be alright.

"Amen."

That's what I probably should have prayed, but I didn't.

What happened is that apparently the Lord had in mind that I should get better at embracing this "silence" thing.

Silence—not a silence I myself chose. That was a litigation-influenced silence. And a silence regarding the precise matters that were causing me all my pain!

Now guess what? I have come to agree with what I observed earlier about Jesus. His thinking that most people had already made up their minds was probably right. If I were to provide a detailed response to all the accusations that were made against me, it probably wouldn't change the minds of those who chose to view us as crooks. And conversely, what I have already written in this book about myself and those closest to me has probably already satisfied our friends and supporters. We are who they always believed us to be. So, I'm inclined to just leave things at that.

In this book I have indirectly given praise and thanks to Jesus for the earthly trials He went through to make it possible for people like me to experience new life in Him.

It is important to put in writing that I am also becoming sensitized to the daily abuse God the Father takes in relative silence. Human beings blame Him for all sorts of problems—"If You're so great, how come You allow people to suffer?" "Why don't You do something, anything, about all the injustices in the world?" "What's up with the weather and all the wars and the wrongdoers?"—as though God the Father is to blame. And He just takes it, for the most part, in silence.

And Holy Spirit, third Person of the blessed Trinity, I praise You as well. You are the One who somehow opens up ears that have long been blocked by the wax of the world. You are unassuming, and yet You are so skilled at what You do.

It took me a bit too long to finally realize it was You who was trying to teach me about sometimes just keeping my mouth shut, and what a benefit that would prove to be. I hope I don't talk as much as I used to, constantly needing to prove myself. Please believe that

I truly want to become someone who is highly sensitive to You, even to Your whispers.

✦ ✦ ✦

It would be unfair for me to leave you with the impression that I have mastered the art of silence and solitude like the Fathers of the Holy Church and the saints of old. The truth is, I think I have a million miles to go to fully understand and experience what I have been sharing about.

True, God has a plan and purpose in our times of silence, whether that silence is by our choice or forced upon us by outside influences.

It's strange, but during this season of trial and grief that we went through as a ministry, there were times when I thought about escaping to a faraway place like Mt. Athos,[9] or becoming like Sadhu Sunder Singh and finding my home in caves so I could just be alone and silent for the rest of my life.

Job of old went into this dark cave of silence when he was cast into chaos and nothing could make any sense of the awful tragedy and pain he had to experience.

King David often confessed his inability to handle the adversity that surrounded him and his longing to fly away like a bird to quietness and rest, if only he could.[10]

Silence can be the most painful thing, or it can be the most beautiful gift when the solitude we escape to is the presence of the eternal, invisible God. When nothing else makes sense and we find ourselves in the maze of chaos, being silent with Him is the greatest refuge.

Looking back, I remember how often I shouted into the silence, saying, "Please stop the train! Let me out!" But no one responded.

I imagine that sounds like self-pity and losing hope. Maybe it was.

Thinking about it more and more, though, I realize that in me there is still the human selfishness and desire for others to understand and approve of me in order to bring some sense of closure.

I want to forget it all and move on with life again. I want to believe all will be fine, yet my emotions are still very raw, and I sometimes find myself crying without even knowing why.

Chaos is not just a theory. It is a living and active thing, like an octopus getting its tentacles wrapped all around you as its grip only gets tighter. But now I also know and have experienced the grace of God and His power, just as Joseph, Daniel and St. Paul experienced it in their earthly journeys with God. So, I say to myself, repeating what St. Paul said to the people at Corinth, "Therefore, since we have this ministry, as we have received mercy, we do not lose heart" (2 Corinthians 4:1).

I think I know now why I am *still* struggling. It's because of this feeling that no matter what I say, some will still not believe me, nor ever choose to be my friend. It grieves me to think of the pain some have gone through and are still going through, believing that they were tricked by us and manipulated.

If you fall into that category, please know, my prayer and hope is that somehow, in some mysterious way, the Holy Spirit will speak to your heart and say to you, "Whatever you did for us, you did it for Christ, and it was worth it."[11] And that makes me glad and brings some closure.

I want to close by repeating the words St. Paul wrote: "My conscience is clear, but that doesn't prove I'm right. It is the Lord himself who will examine me and decide" (1 Corinthians 4:4–5, NLT).

I wait, and *I must*, for "the world's last night"[12] as C.S. Lewis put it, and then "the Son of Righteousness will rise with healing in His wings."[13] Till then I must press on.

I invite you to join with me on this journey of faith, never giving up until we see His face.

Maran-a´tha.[14]

NOTES

Front Matter

Introduction

1. "The Tales That Really Mattered...," *The Lord of the Rings: The Two Towers,* special extended ed. Directed by Peter Jackson (2002; Los Angeles, CA: New Line Home Entertainment, 2003), DVD.

1. See 2 Corinthians 11:28.

Chapter 1: Cast into Chaos

1. Rosemary Ellen Guiley, comp., *The Quotable Saint* (New York, NY: Facts on File, Inc., 2002), p. 49.

2. See Ephesians 6:12.

3. Robert Frost, *New Hampshire, Stopping by the Woods on a Snowy Evening,* lines 14–15 (New York, NY: Henry Holt, 1923). Public Domain.

4. See Job 1:1–5.

5. Job 1:8.

6. Job 2:9.

7. See Job 1:1–2:10.

8. See 1 Kings 19:1–4.

9. http://www.christianashram.org/e-stanley-jones.html. (Accessed January 10, 2020).

10. *Mother Teresa: In My Own Words*, ed. José Luis González-Balado, (Liguori, MO: Liguori Publications, 1997), p. 91.
11. C.S. Lewis, *A Grief Observed* (New York, NY: HarperCollins Publishers, 1994), p. 14.
12. *Before and After,* directed by Barbet Schroeder (1996; Minneapolis, MN: Mill Creek Entertainment, 2004), DVD.
13. See 1 Timothy 1:15.
14. Lewis, *A Grief Observed,* pp. 6–7.
15. See St. Luke 18:13, paraphrased.
16. Lewis, *A Grief Observed,* p. 3.
17. C.S. Lewis, *The Lion, the Witch and the Wardrobe* (New York, NY: Macmillan Publishing Company, 1970).
18. K.P. Yohannan, *No Longer a Slumdog,* rev. ed. (Wills Point, TX: GFA Books, 2017).
19. See Psalm 73.
20. See Romans 8:28–29.

Chapter 2: Deep in the Forest Fire

1. *The Collected Works of St. Teresa of Avila, Vol. 2,* comps. Kieran Kavanaugh and Otilio Rodriguez, (Washington, DC: ICB Publications, 2012) pp. 419–420.
2. C.S. Lewis, *Mere Christianity* (New York, NY: HarperCollins Publishers, 2001), p. 46.
3. 2 Corinthians 5:14.
4. See Exodus 1:15–22.
5. See Judges 16.
6. See 1 Kings 19.
7. See Esther 3:1–7:10.
8. See St. Matthew 26:14–16.
9. Paul Lane, *Viral News on Social Media* (New York, NY: The Rosen Publishing Group, Inc., 2019), p. 14.
10. P.W. Singer and Emerson T. Brooking, *LikeWar: The Weaponization of Social Media* (New York, NY: Houghton Mifflin Harcourt Publishing Company, 2018), p. 122.
11. Singer and Brooking, *LikeWar: The Weaponization of Social Media,* p. 123.

12. Romans 12:14.
13. See Galatians 6:1.
14. Daniel 3:19, NLT.

Chapter 3: Suffering Is the Way of Life

1. Father Joseph Irvin, *The Church Fathers Speak,* Illustrated ed. (n.p., n.d.), POD, Coppell, TX, January 3, 2020, pp. 161–162.
2. See 2 Corinthians 1:15–22; 2 Corinthians 6:11–13; 2 Corinthians 7:5–7; 2 Corinthians11:7–11; 2 Corinthians 11:23–27.
3. K.P. Yohannan, *Touching Godliness* (Wills Point, TX: GFA Books, 2013).
4. See 2 Corinthians 10:1–12:21.
5. See St. Mark 6:1–6.
6. See Philippians 1:29.
7. See Exodus 15:22–27.
8. See the Acts of the Apostles 20:17–25; Philippians 1:21.
9. The Acts of the Apostles 7:60, paraphrased.
10. See the Acts of the Apostles 9:1–31.
11. Paul Burns, *Butler's Lives of the Saints* (Collegeville, MN: Liturgical Press, 2003), p. 213.
12. Johannes Jörgensen, *Saint Francis of Assisi: A Biography,* trans. T. O'Conor Sloane (New York: Longmans, Green, and Co., 1912), p. 160.
13. 2 Corinthians 4:10–11.
14. See 2 Corinthians 11:23–29.
15. See 1 Corinthians 10:31.
16. The Acts of the Apostles 4:31.
17. Hebrews 5:8, NLT.
18. See Philippians 2:6–8.
19. Ray C. Stedman, *Talking With My Father* (Grand Rapids, MI: Discovery House Publishers, 1997), p. 27–28.
20. St. Luke 22:31–33, paraphrased.
21. See Isaiah 55:8–9.
22. See Psalm 103:7.

Chapter 4: My Journey to Ancient Paths

1. A.W. Tozer, *The Pursuit of God* (Abbotsford, WI: Life Sentence Publishing, Inc., 2015), p. 13.

2. https://biography.yourdictionary.com/clement-i (Accessed January 10, 2020); https://www.britannica.com/biography/St-Ignatius-of-Antioch (Accessed January 10, 2020); https://www.loyolapress.com/our-catholic-faith/saints/saints-stories-for-all-ages/saint-polycarp. (Accessed January 10, 2020).

3. Burns, *Butler's Lives of the Saints,* p. 107.

4. James S. Cutsinger, comp., ed., *Not of This World: A Treasure of Christian Mysticism* (Bloomington, IN: World Wisdom Inc., 2003), p. 27.

5. Everett Ferguson, *Church History, Vol. 1: From Christ to Pre-Reformation* (Grand Rapids, MI: Zondervan, 2005). See chap. 10, "Diocletian and Constantine: On the Threshold of the Fourth Century."

6. See 1 John 2:6.

7. Henri Nouwen, *The Way of the Heart: The Spirituality of the Desert Fathers and Mothers* (New York, NY: HarperCollins Publishers, 1981).

8. St. Athanasius, *The Life of Saint Antony,* trans. Robert T. Meyer, (Mahwah, NJ: Paulist Press, 1978).

9. Athanasius Yohan, *Theosis,* Faith and Tradition Series (Thiruvalla, India: Believers Eastern Church Synod Secretariat, 2018).

10. See Job 33:14–18; Acts 2:17.

11. Vladimir Lossky, *The Mystical Theology of the Eastern Church,* trans. Fellowship of St Alban and St Sergius (UK) (Cambridge, UK: James Clarke & Co., Ltd., 1991).

12. W. Ian Thomas, *The Saving Life of Christ* and *The Mystery of Godliness,* Clarion Classics (Grand Rapids, MI: Zondervan Publishing House, 1988).

13. Timothy Ware, *The Orthodox Church,* rev. ed. (London, UK: Penguin Books Ltd., 1997), p. 21.

14. C.S. Lewis, *Mere Christianity,* pp. 205–206.

15. Sadhu Sundar Singh, *Visions of the World: A Brief Description of the Spiritual Realm, Its Different States of Existence, and the Destiny of Good and Evil Men as Seen in Visions,* (n.p., 1926). POD, Coppell, TX, December 18, 2019.

16. "Journey to the Sky - Sadhu Sundar Singh," YouTube video, 41:45, posted by "BRMinistries," January 24, 2014, https://www.youtube.com/watch?v=WzKjj-gOo-Q. (Accessed January 10, 2020).

17. See Genesis 1:26.

18. See St. Matthew 26:34, 16:18.

19. See St. John 8:1–11.

20. St. John 6:53, paraphrased.

21. Revelation 13:8, paraphrased.

22. David Kinnaman and Aly Hawkins, *You Lost Me: Why Young Christians Are Leaving Church, and Rethinking Faith* (Grand Rapids, MI: Baker Books, 2016), p. 23.

23. St. James 5:14–16, paraphrased.

24. See 2 Samuel 12:1–15.

25. See 2 Samuel 12:1–15; St. Luke 15:11–31; 1 John 1:8–9.

26. http://ww1.antiochian.org/content/confession-healing-sacrament. (Accessed January 10, 2020).

27. St. John 20:23.

28. Athanasius Yohan, *Who Am I?* Faith and Tradition Series (Thiruvalla, India: Believers Eastern Church Publications, 2018).

29. See Isaiah 57:15.

Chapter 5: Another Link in the Chain

1. Ted Schroder, *Buried Treasure* (Amelia Island, FL: Amelia Island Publishing, Inc., 2005), p. 217.

2. https://www.newworldencyclopedia.org/entry/Bishop. (Accessed January 10, 2020).

3. See Romans 10:14–15.

4. See St. Matthew 28:18–20; Acts 1:8.

5. See the Acts of the Apostles 15:1–41.

6. See St. Matthew 16:18.

7. Athanasius Yohan, *Holy Tradition*, Faith and Tradition Series (Thiruvalla, India: Believers Eastern Church Synod Secretariat, 2019).

8. K.P. Yohannan, *Revolution in World Missions*, rev. ed. (Wills Point, TX: GFA Books, 2017), p. 27.

9. See 2 Corinthians 11:2; 2 Thessalonians 2:15.

10. The Acts of the Apostles 15:28.

11. Robert E. Webber, *Common Roots: The Original Call to an Ancient-Future Faith* (Grand Rapids, MI: Zondervan, 2009).

12. Ferguson, *Church History, Vol. 1: From Christ to Pre-Reformation*, p. 396.

13. John D. Woodbridge and Frank A. James III, *Church History, Vol. II: From Pre-Reformation to the Present Day* (Grand Rapids, MI: Zondervan, 2013), pp. 218–227.

14. Hank Hanegraaff, *Truth Matters, Life Matters More: The Unexpected Beauty of an Authentic Christian Life* (Nashville, TN: W Publishing, 2019), p. 127.

15. Dr. K.P. Yohannan Metropolitan, *Guiding Principles*, Faith and Tradition Series, 6th ed., rev. (Thiruvalla, India: Believers Eastern Church Publications, 2018).

16. See the Acts of the Apostles 2:1–47.

17. See the Acts of the Apostles 13:1–3.

18. http://www.naute.com/stories/3stonecutters.php. (Accessed January 10, 2020).

19. See St. Matthew 28:18–20.

20. See Romans 15:20.

21. See the Acts of the Apostles 20:28.

22. Erwin Fahlbusch et. al., *The Encyclopedia of Christianity Vol. 4, P-Sh*, trans. Geoffrey W. Bromiley (Grand Rapids, MI: Wm. B. Eerdmans Publishing Company, 2005), p. 157.

23. See Ephesians 5:25–27.

24. 1 John 4:8.

25. See Jeremiah 6:16.

Chapter 6: Hunger for Reality

1. *The Essential Wisdom of the Saints,* comp. Carol Kelly-Gangi (New York, NY: Fall River Press, 2008), p. 43.
2. Naftali Bendavid, "Europe's Empty Churches Go on Sale," *The Wall Street Journal,* January 2, 2015. https://www.wsj.com/articles/europes-empty-churches-go-on-sale-1420245359. (Accessed January 10, 2020).; Lauren Schuker Blum, "Religious Conversions," *The Wall Street Journal,* December 13, 2012. https://www.wsj.com/articles/SB100014241278873240011045781633037536 32508. (Accessed January 10, 2020).
3. See 2 Thessalonians 2:1–3.
4. https://www.christianpost.com/news/20-beheaded-coptic-christians-who-did-not-renounce-faith-in-jesus-before-isis-finally-laid-to-rest.html. (Accessed July 26, 2019).
5. See Revelation 5:6.
6. See 2 Corinthians 11:4.
7. See Genesis 1:26.
8. See Romans 8:29.
9. See 2 Corinthians 3:18.
10. Ware, *The Orthodox Church,* p. 21.
11. Ware, *The Orthodox Church,* p. 232.
12. See 2 Corinthians 4:16.
13. See Romans 12:1.
14. Ware, *The Orthodox Church, pp. 231–232.* The text relating to deification was largely based on this source.
15. See Philippians 2:5–9.
16. See Philippians 2:6–8.
17. St. John 14:9.
18. Genesis 1:27.
19. Exodus 3:6.
20. Revelation 12:10.
21. George Verwer, *Messiology: The Mystery of How God Works Even When It Doesn't Make Sense to Us,* rev. ed. (Chicago, IL: Moody Publishers, 2016).

22. St. John 17:21, paraphrased.

23. See St. John 13:35.

24. William MacDonald, *True Discipleship,* rev. ed. (Port Colborne, Canada: Gospel Folio Press, 2003).; see also Dietrich Bonhoeffer, *The Cost of Discipleship,* rev. ed., trans. R.H. Fuller (London, UK: SCM Press, 2015).

25. See 2 Corinthians 11:4.

26. See Philippians 3:4.

27. See Philippians 3:9.

28. See Jeremiah 18:1–11.

29. See St. John 15:1–17.

30. Watchman Nee, *The Release of the Spirit* (New York: Christian Fellowship Publishers, Inc., 2000).

31. See St. John 21:15–25.

32. See Galatians 5:15.

33. See St. Matthew 16:24–26.

34. C.S. Lewis, *God in the Dock: Essays on Theology and Ethics,* ed. Walter Hooper (Grand Rapids, MI: William B. Eerdmans Publishing Company, 2014).

35. See the Acts of the Apostles 20:29.

36. See Hebrews 12:2.

Chapter 7: Look-Alikes

1. A.W. Tozer, *I Talk Back to the Devil* (Chicago, IL: Moody Publishers, 2018), p. 32.

2. St. Matthew 7:12.

3. See St. Mark 12:31.

4. See 2 Corinthians 11:14.

5. See Hebrews 12:1–2.

6. See Galatians 1:8; 1 Timothy 6:3–5.

7. Dr. K.P. Yohannan Metropolitan, *The Plumb Line,* Faith and Tradition Series (Tiruvalla, India: Believers Eastern Church Synod Secretariat, 2017).

8. Bruce M. Metzger, *The Canon of the New Testament: Its Origin, Development, and Significance* (New York: Oxford University Press Inc., 1997).

9. See Romans 8:29; 1 Corinthians. 3:18.

10. See Acts of the Apostles 13:1–13.

11. See Isaiah 6:1–8.

12. See Nehemiah 8:4–9.

13. See St. Luke 11:28; 1 Timothy. 4:13.

14. Henry R. Percival, ed. *The Seven Ecumenical Councils of the Undivided Church* (Oxford: Benediction Classics, 2011).

15. Definition taken from https://www.merriam-webster.com/dictionary/source. (Accessed January 10, 2020).

16. Psalm 42:1.

17. 2 Peter 1:4.

18. Yohan, *Holy Tradition.*

19. https://www.britannica.com/topic/Pharisee. (Accessed January 10, 2020).

20. See 1 Corinthians 10:31.

21. See 1 John 2:6.

22. See the Acts of the Apostles 2:42.

23. St. John 6:53.

24. 1 Thessalonians 4:17.

25. See Isaiah 6:1–4; Revelation 4:1–5:14.

26. Psalm 50:5, paraphrased.

27. Genesis 49:10, KJV.

28. The Acts of the Apostles 8:4, NLT.

29. The Acts of the Apostles 5:20, paraphrased.

30. See St. Matthew 5:13–16.

31. See 2 Corinthians 1:4.

32. St. Luke 19:10.

33. See Ezekiel 16:49–50.

34. Richard Stewart, *Leper Priest of Moloka'i: The Father Damien Story* (Honolulu: University of Hawai'i Press, 2000).

35. Hebrews 13:8.

36. See St. Matthew 25:35–40.

37. St. John 9:4.

Chapter 8: Beginning of the End

1. Revelation 10:6, WYC.
2. "George Burns - 'I wish I was 18 again'," YouTube video, 4:28, posted by "Bob Young," March 17, 2011, https://www.youtube.com/watch?v=M57__OyMCfI. (Accessed January 10, 2020).
3. See Ecclesiastes 6:10–12; Hebrews 9:27.
4. See St. Luke 22:42; St. John 6:38, 14:31.
5. C.S. Lewis, *The Silver Chair* (New York, NY: Macmillan Publishing Company, 1970), p. 21.
6. See 1 John 3:2.
7. See the Acts of the Apostles 20:17–24, paraphrased.
8. St. Matthew 10:16, NLT.
9. See St. John 16:33; St. Matthew 28:20.
10. See Isaiah 40:31; Revelation 4:1.
11. See Psalm 139:7; Matthew 28:20; Hebrews 13:5.
12. 2 Corinthians 4:1, paraphrased.
13. Ruth A. Tucker, *From Jerusalem to Irian Jaya: A Biographical History of Christian Missions,* 2nd ed. (Grand Rapids, MI: Zondervan, 2004), p. 357.
14. John F. Thornton and Susan B. Varenne, ed., *The Book of Job* (New York: Vintage Books, 1998).
15. St. Matthew 16:24–26, paraphrased.
16. See St. Matthew 11:28.

Chapter 9: One Minute to Midnight

1. C.S. Lewis, *The Business of Heaven,* ed. Walter Hooper (San Francisco: HarperOne, 2017), p. 149.
2. Yohannan, *Revolution in World Missions.*
3. Yohannan, *No Longer a Slumdog.*
4. See St. Luke 22:31.
5. See Genesis 12:1–2.
6. See Exodus 7:16.
7. See Jeremiah 1:1–6:30.
8. 2 Peter 1:19–21.
9. See St. Luke 21:36.
10. See Daniel 12:10.

11. Dietrich Bonhoeffer, *Life Together* (New York, NY: Harper-Collins Publishers, 1954).

12. See St. Matthew 24:6–7.

13. See St. Matthew 24:22.

14. See St. Matthew 24:7; Revelation 6:6–8.

15. See 2 Peter 3:11.

16. See Revelation 12:12.

17. Genesis 19:17.

18. Rod Dreher, *The Benedict Option: A Strategy for Christians in a Post-Christian Nation* (New York, NY: Sentinel, 2017).

19. Ibid, p. 3.

20. https://www.taize.fr/en. (Accessed January 10, 2020).

21. See St. Mark 11:24; Romans 10:17.

Chapter 10: Silence

1. *The Essential Wisdom of the Saints,* comp. Carol Kelly-Gangi, p. 29.

2. See Exodus 34:28; Isaiah 6:1–13; St. Matthew 4:1–11.

3. See 1 Corinthians 3:12–13.

4. Watchman Nee, *The Release of the Spirit.*

5. "Asleep in the Light - Keith Green (Legendado)," YouTube video, 4:46, posted by "Eduardo Carniel," August 9, 2010, https://www.youtube.com/watch?v=W2AD68ObUm8. (Accessed January 10, 2020).

6. See St. Matthew 3:1.

7. See St. Matthew 4:1–2.

8. See St. Mark 6:46; St. Luke 5:16.

9. http://mountathosinfos.gr/. (Accessed January 10, 2020).

10. See Psalm 55:6.

11. See St. Matthew 25:40.

12. C.S. Lewis, *The World's Last Night: And Other Essays* (San Francisco: HarperOne, 2017).

13. Malachi 4:2.

14. See Revelation 22:12.

Watch these videos at NeverGiveUpBook.org

A pastor shares about seeing the ministry on the field and meeting his Bridge of Hope child

Supporters see firsthand the impact of their gift

Watch an in-depth interview between Pastor Francis Chan and author Dr. K.P. Yohannan

NeverGiveUpBook.org

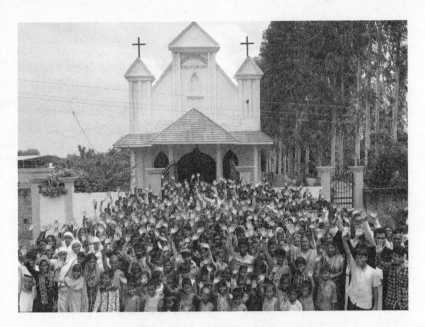

GFA World is *your* bridge to bringing the hope of Christ to those who still wait to hear His name.

Join us in building up the Holy Church around the world!

It's been 2,000 years since Christ walked the earth, yet nearly 2 billion people have not heard the news that God loves them. How long must they wait?

This is why GFA World exists.

More than 40 years ago, God specifically called us to invest our lives in proclaiming His all-embracing love to our generation, especially in nations that have not had a chance to hear about Christ. Today, there are thousands of congregations spread throughout so many nations that are worshiping and following the Lord because faithful workers are serving full time so others may finally know God's love.

Because these national workers serve within and around their own cultures, this natural advantage makes them one of the most effective means to tangibly share the Good News.

However, the economically weak churches in these developing nations can't do it alone. The enormous task of sharing the love of Christ with nearly 2 billion people takes the partnership of the Church worldwide.

GFA offers those who cannot go themselves the opportunity to **become senders and prayer partners** of these national workers.

Together, we can help fulfill the Great Commission!

Find more info about GFA World and get a copy of K.P. Yohannan's book *Revolution in World Missions* by visiting our website, www.gfa.org, or contacting one of our offices near you.

Contact Information

For more information contact the organization nearest you.

AUSTRALIA: GFA World Inc, PO Box 3587, Toowoomba QLD 4350
Freephone: 1300 889 339 • infoau@gfa.org • www.gfaau.org

CANADA: GFA World, 245 King Street E, Stoney Creek, ON L8G 1L9
Toll-free: 1-888-946-2742 • info@gfa.ca • www.gfa.ca

FINLAND: GFA World Finland ry, PL 63, FI-65101, Vaasa
Phone: 358 50 036 96 99 • infofi@gfa.org • www.gfa.fi

GERMANY: GFA World (e.V.), Am Sodenmatt 28, 28259 Bremen
Phone: 0421 5961 9091 • info@gfaworld.de • www.gfaworld.de

KOREA: GFA Korea, Seok-Am Blg 5F, 6-9, Teheran-ro 25-gil,
Gangnam-gu, Seoul, 06132, Republic of Korea
Tel: 02-6279-7798 • infokorea@gfa.or.kr • gfa.or.kr

NEW ZEALAND: GFA World, PO Box 302580, North Harbour, Auckland 0751
Toll-free: 0800-819-819 • info@gfa.org.nz • www.gfa.org.nz

SOUTH AFRICA: GFA (SA), P.O. Box 28880, Sunridge Park, Port Elizabeth 6008
Phone: 041 360-0198 • infoza@gfa.org • www.gospelforasia.org.za

UNITED KINGDOM: GFA World (U.K.), PO Box 316, Manchester M22 2DJ
Phone: 0161 946 9484 • infouk@gfa.org • www.gfauk.org

UNITED STATES: GFA, Inc., 1116 St. Thomas Way, Wills Point, TX 75169
Toll-free: 1-800-946-2742 • info@gfa.org • www.gfa.org

GFA World is taking the love of Christ to those who have lived their lives without ever hearing Christ's name. We are bringing joy and hope to destitute widows, orphans, leprosy patients, suffering children and families in extreme poverty.

Partner with GFA World:

- Make a donation to GFA World
- Choose a national missionary to sponsor
- Sponsor a child with your birthday

Visit
NeverGiveUpBook.org/Partner

For $1 a day, you can sponsor a missionary or needy child from one of many nations. Find out today how simple it is to make a lasting difference!

Be Part of the Answer

You can make a tremendous difference in the lives of countless people when you become part of the GFA World team! Check out these opportunities:

Serve at GFA World
» Use your God-given talents and skills by serving full time at a GFA World office. There's a list of opportunities located on our website you can apply for!

Volunteer for GFA World
» Engage with the people in your community to see lives transformed around the globe.

Join GFA's School of Discipleship
» Pursue God in this one-year program for single adults between the ages of 18–27. It's sure to be a turning point in your life.

By giving your life to serve the Lord, you can help enable thousands of national workers to fulfill the Great Commission.

Learn more about becoming part of the answer:

NeverGiveUpBook.org/Answer